WJEC
CBAC

WJEC GCSE
ENGLISH
LANGUAGE
AIMING FOR A-A*

ROGER LANE

OXFORD
UNIVERSITY PRESS

OXFORD
UNIVERSITY PRESS

Great Clarendon Street, Oxford OX2 6DP

Oxford University Press is a department of the University of Oxford.
It furthers the University's objective of excellence in research,
scholarship, and education by publishing worldwide in

Oxford   New York

Auckland   Cape Town   Dar es Salaam   Hong Kong   Karachi
Kuala Lumpur   Madrid   Melbourne   Mexico City   Nairobi
New Delhi   Shanghai   Taipei   Toronto

With offices in

Argentina   Austria   Brazil   Chile   Czech Republic   France   Greece
Guatemala   Hungary   Italy   Japan   Poland   Portugal   Singapore
South Korea   Switzerland   Thailand   Turkey   Ukraine   Vietnam

Oxford is a registered trade mark of Oxford University Press
in the UK and in certain other countries

British Library Cataloguing in Publication Data

Data available

ISBN 978-0-19-913621-6

10 9 8 7 6 5 4 3 2 1

Printed in Great Britain by Bell and Bain Ltd., Glasgow

Author's acknowledgements
Grateful thanks to Wayne Powell, who understands
people, language and history; An unsung WJEC hero
and a long-time friend.
Thanks again to Nicola Dutton for her support and to
Hayley Cox and the team for all the professionalism
in Oxford.

CONTENTS

INTRODUCTION

SECTION 1: READING

SECTION 2: WRITING

SECTION 3: SPOKEN LANGUAGE

Features OF THIS BOOK

This book provides lots of useful features to help you stretch your skills and develop your understanding, as you progress through your GCSE English Language course. Here is a quick guide to what you can expect:

Feedback from other students
Find out what other students think about English Language; what they have found challenging and approaches they have taken to improve their work.

Sample student answers
Annotated student answers give examples of top-grade writing with comments from the examiner.

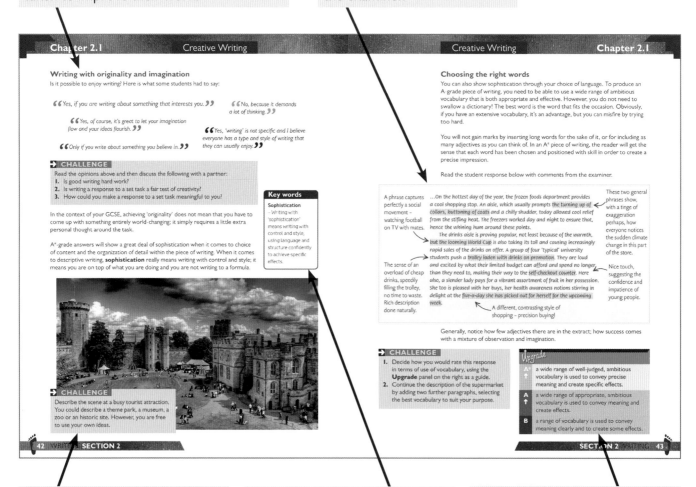

Challenge activity boxes
This book is filled with challenging activities to help you broaden your skills and improve your understanding of English Language.

Key words
Key word boxes provide definitions of important terms from the Assessment Objectives and marking criteria, to help you understand what you need to do to reach the top grades.

Upgrade panels
These colour-coded panels show you what is expected of a grade B, A or A* answer and help you to understand the differences between these grades.

Upgrade

Throughout the book and at the end of every chapter, you will find colour-coded **Upgrade panels**. This feature is designed to help you improve your work and move up through the grades. Each panel focuses on a particular part of the assessment and explains what is expected of a grade B, A and A* answer.

Upgrade

A* ↑	a wide range of well-judged, ambitious vocabulary is used to convey precise meaning and create specific effects.
A ↑	a wide range of appropriate, ambitious vocabulary is used to convey meaning and create effects.
B	a range of vocabulary is used to convey meaning clearly and to create some effects.

Small Upgrade panels

The panel on the left focuses on the use of vocabulary in creative writing. Small panels like this appear throughout each chapter. These panels may be linked to other features on the page such as activities, sample tasks and sample answers.

Full-page Upgrade panels

At the end of each chapter, you will find a full-page Upgrade panel. This is designed to help you assess your own practice answers and extended writing.

At the end of each chapter you will find a practice task to complete. When attempting the practice tasks, try to limit yourself to the time you would have available in the real assessment. Once you have completed it, you can use the Upgrade panel to rate your work. You can then work out what you need to do to improve your performance.

Upgrade self-assessment panels
Full page self-assessment panels help you to rate your work and identify where you can improve.

Practice exam questions
Based on the format of real exam papers and Controlled Assessment tasks, these practice questions allow you to test what you have learned.

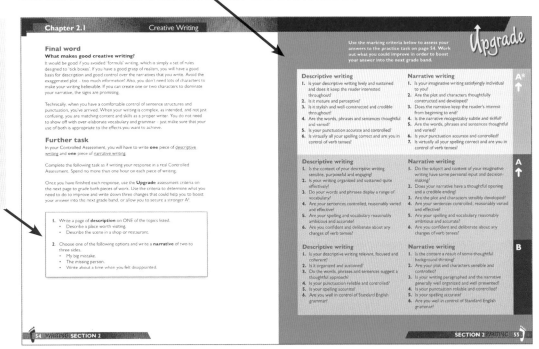

Chapter 1.1   Non-Fiction texts

Aim for A

- Your answers show that you have a comfortable overview of each of the set texts and they also get to grips with the detail.
- You have a clear understanding of the attitude of the writer in each text.
- When writing about persuasive techniques, you are able to comment on key features and link them confidently to the meaning of the texts.
- When comparing texts, your points are coherent and well organized.

Aim for A*

- You are able to move smoothly from an overview to the detail of the texts.
- You have understood and communicated the attitude and intentions of the writers in each text.
- When writing about persuasive techniques, you are able to build your ideas into a successful argument.
- When comparing texts, your points are coherent, perceptive and highly organized.

Reading non-fiction

Reading non-fiction texts in the exam means answering questions with some skill on journalistic writing, autobiographical or biographical writing and other types of non-fiction texts like promotional or documentary texts. You need to explore and analyse the texts confidently, by engaging with the writer's ideas and opinions. You need to select and highlight key details, but you also need a good grasp of each writer's **purpose** and motivation for writing.

At the top level, spotting features is not enough. You must deal with the perspectives and the arguments offered in the texts, making comments and showing that you are aware of the tone of the writing through your own choice of expression.

As well as answering questions on a single text, you will also need to show that you can compare texts efficiently. As well as identifying differences in content and approach, top-grade students will be just as adept at probing and comparing the intentions of different writers and will be able to explain these ideas with clarity and coherence.

> ## Key words
>
> **Purpose** – To identify the purpose of a text you need to work out why the writer decided to write it and what he or she hopes to achieve by it. What does the writer want the reader to do or think?

THE ASSESSMENT

GCSE English Language Unit 1

This unit will be assessed by an **exam** lasting **one hour**. The exam will test reading and responding to language, layout and pictures. You will be given **two** non-fiction texts in the exam and you will be asked a series of questions on them. One of the questions, probably the final one, will be a question requiring the comparison of both texts.

What you should and should not do

Do

- take the full 60 minutes and spread your time wisely between questions.
- focus on the key words of each question.
- read each text to gain a full understanding of each writer's purpose and argument.
- say the obvious and important things first, then move on quickly.
- pile in the evidence, where required, using your own words wherever possible.
- explain only when you need to.
- quote short whenever you can, but quote a phrase or even a sentence, if necessary.
- use words like *maybe*, *possibly*, *probably*, when something is uncertain or open for debate, but also respond honestly and directly when something is shocking or funny or moving.

Don't

- waste words.
- expect the same points to be rewarded twice in your answer.
- write vague, empty comments about long sentences, short sentences and commas.
- write meaningless, general comments about headlines, pictures and layout.

Identifying implied meanings

To write an A*-grade answer you need to show that you can identify implied meanings and recognize the intentions of the writer by reading between the lines.

Read the short extracts, below, about the city of São Paulo in Brazil. The purpose of the exercise is to focus your attention on the details of each text through considering the meaning and implications of each sentence in turn. You can then start to show your deeper understanding of the texts by using your own words.

Text 1

São Paulo is the largest city in Brazil, with a city population of about 11 million and almost 20 million in its metropolitan region. It is the capital of the southeastern state of São Paulo, and also a beehive of activity that offers a jovial nightlife and an intense cultural experience. São Paulo is one of the richest cities in the southern hemisphere, though inequality between the classes typically observed in Brazil is blatant.

Text 2

SÃO PAULO, or Sampa as it is also often called, is probably one of the most underrated cities tourism-wise, often shaded by other places in the Brazilian sun and beach circuit such as Rio de Janeiro and Salvador. It is in fact a great city to explore, with its own idiosyncrasies, the exquisite way of living of its inhabitants, not to mention the world-class restaurants and diverse regional and international cuisine available to all tastes. If there is a major attraction to this city, it is the excellent quality of its restaurants and the variety of cultural activities on display.

Consider the first sentence in **Text 1** above. How might you make a confident and convincing statement of your own about the size of São Paulo as presented in this extract?

Rather than repeat the words of the writer ('largest city…', 'about 11 million…'), you could convey a more alert understanding by noting that 'São Paulo is *huge*, and it is particularly *densely populated* in its city centre'.

→ **CHALLENGE**

1. Look at the second sentence of **Text 1**. Write a sentence giving your impressions of São Paulo.
2. Explain in your own words what you learn about São Paulo from the third and final sentence of the text.

→ **CHALLENGE**

1. Now, look at **Text 2**. Explain, in your own words, the writer's view of São Paulo, as expressed in the first sentence.
2. How does the writer portray São Paulo in the second sentence?
3. Comment on the impact and effect of the third sentence.

Comparing texts

Working with the detail of your texts is important, but so is obtaining an overall view. This is especially important when comparing texts. The best answers will grasp the overriding differences before getting involved with the details.

Typically, the comparison question will prompt you to write your comparison from a particular angle, focusing, for example, on the <u>views</u> of each writer or the <u>methods</u> the writers use to influence the reader.

When writing your answer, don't waffle. Thoughtful reading needs careful expression. You do not always need quotations. Sometimes an obsession with quoting can prevent students from properly exploring the texts. Organization and balance are critical in a top-grade comparison. Use sentences like: 'Both the article and the leaflet...' and 'The article..., whereas the leaflet...'

Avoid ⚠

Do not ignore the bigger picture. What effect does the whole text have on you? What's going on? Work with the details but remember to step back occasionally and take a broader view.

→ **CHALLENGE**

Write a paragraph in response to the following task:
Compare the writers' views of São Paulo in **Text 1** and **Text 2**.

Writing about longer texts

Having completed a mini-task on reading non-fiction, you are now going to embark on a full-scale reading challenge. Here, as in the exam, you will tackle two texts on a related topic.

Firstly, read the newspaper report, below, on the 'Action for Happiness' movement. As you read it, work out what this organization is trying to do, and what the writer of the report thinks of it. In other words, keep your brain in gear while you are reading!

'Action for Happiness' movement launches with free hugs and love

Alexandra Topping

Members pledge to replace self-obsessed materialism with caring action groups at work, home and in the community.

Passers-by enjoy free hugs outside the London launch of the 'Action for Happiness' movement.

As drivers angrily beeped their horns and cyclists weaved impatiently through London's traffic, Amandeep Hothi stood cheerily on the pavement holding aloft a sign offering, in pink letters, "Free Hugs".

Hothi is part of a new group called 'Action for Happiness', whose members aim to boost the net amount of joy in the world by being kind to others and countering "an epidemic of loneliness and isolation".

The movement was launched yesterday at Jerwood Hall in the City of London, where the movement's co-founder told attendees – who wore badges with slogans such as "Love more!" and "I'm up for more happiness!" – that they could "turn the rising tide of excessive individualism".

"Despite the fact that we are getting richer, after 60 years we still haven't managed to produce a happier society," said Professor Richard Layard, head of the wellbeing programme at the London School of Economics. "We are asking people for an individual commitment to aim to produce more happiness and less misery."

"The time is right. There is a worldwide hunger for something better, and we believe we can harness it," he added.

The movement's supporters say it is not just about fluffy slogans or interfering do-gooders. Founded last year, it requires members, who can sign up via a website, to set up action groups to promote happiness wherever possible: at work, at home or in the community.

There is evidence that the happiness movement is being taken seriously in high places. As deep public-sector cuts loomed, David Cameron told a conference last year that it was time "we admitted that there's more to life than money", adding: "It's time we focused not just on GDP but on GWB – general wellbeing."

In November, the government asked the Office of National Statistics to produce measures to gauge "general wellbeing". France's president, Nicolas Sarkozy, has declared his intention to include happiness and wellbeing in France's measurement of economic progress, while Canadian statisticians also poll subjective wellbeing across the country.

The launch, hosted by TV presenter Sian Williams, was followed by a group meditation only briefly disturbed by a determined ringtone. Action for Happiness's director, Mark Williamson, rallied the troops. Britain was in an "epidemic of loneliness and isolation" but research showed helping others, as well as having a positive effect on your own wellbeing, could have a far-reaching impact, he said.

"The contagious nature of happiness means that we affect not only our friends, but our friends' friends. It spreads to form an extremely powerful social network."

The Action for Happiness website yesterday collapsed under the weight of users, declaring itself overwhelmed – a reminder, perhaps, that the search for contentment is sometimes beyond our control.

→ **CHALLENGE**

In pairs, discuss the sample exam question below and the sample answers that follow. What is the exam question asking students to focus on? Which answer do you think is the most effective?

Look at the 'Action for Happiness' article.

1. Explain how and why the 'Action for Happiness' movement has been launched. [10]

Sample answer 1

The Action for Happiness movement has been launched to cheer up people and make the world a better place, by giving free hugs to people that need them. Action for Happiness "aim to boost the net amount of joy in the world by being kind to others"; this shows that Action for Happiness care about other people's feelings and they want the world to be a better place. Action for Happiness is trying to spread the love by wearing badges that say "Love more!" and "I'm up for more happiness". This means that despite how mush hatred there is in the world, they are trying their best to cover it up by spreading love. Action for Happiness is trying to find people partners and they think it might make people love more. It says they could "turn the rising tide of excessive individualism". This suggests that Action for Happiness can find two single people and let them love each other.

Sample answer 2

Action for Happiness was launched to discourage people from being selfish and materialistic. It launched with a website and a publicity stunt of free hugs on the street, but its serious intention is to encourage people to join 'caring' groups in the community. It believes that being kind to others and promoting happiness will boost the amount of joy in society generally and reduce the amount of loneliness. At the same time, some people are too individual and if you help others it will have a positive effect on you as well. Even the Prime Minister says there is more to life than money.

→ **CHALLENGE**

1. Use the **Upgrade** panel, below, to mark each answer by crediting words, phrases and sentences as appropriate.
2. Why is **Sample Answer 2** more successful than **Sample Answer 1**?

Upgrade

A*↑	answers make a range of valid points and are thorough and coherent, showing a depth of understanding and a confident overview.
A↑	answers select a range of valid points, show a clear focus on the question and give a sense of coherence.
B	answers select and explain a range of valid points.

Read the next sample exam question on the 'Action for Happiness' article and look critically at the student answer that follows.

> **2.** How does the writer of the article try to interest and engage the reader? Think about:
>
> - the use of the headline and picture   • what is said   • how it is said.
>
> [10]

The article interests you by the use of the picture. When you see the article, the first thing you see is the image of two people hugging. It makes you wonder why they are hugging and what has made a miserable society into a happier society. This image makes you want to start reading the rest of the article and see what's happening. Another reason why the article is interesting is the title: "Action for Happiness movement launches with free hugs and love". The title makes it sound more fun. The writer has used the word 'free' and many members of the British public get engaged when something free is offered. As Britain is still in recession, the amazement of free things is really great. This makes the reader very engaged.

This exam question asks you to comment on how the writer uses linguistic, grammatical, structural and presentational features to engage the reader, to achieve effects and to influence the reader.

→ CHALLENGE

1. Use the **Upgrade** panel below to determine what mark you would give the student response.
2. What prevents this answer from achieving the next grade and what could this student do to improve the answer?

Upgrade

A* ↑	answers should combine specific detail with overview and fully engage with the techniques used to interest the reader. Answers should also include an exploration of the effect of presentational and structural features.
A ↑	answers should explore the text in detail and make valid comments and inferences. Answers should include reference to the effect of presentational and structural features.
B	answers should address the issue of 'how', although they may rely on some spotting of key facts or quotations. Better answers will have a clear focus on techniques used to engage the reader, including exploration of the effect of presentational and structural features.

> ### → CHALLENGE
>
> 1. In relation to the 'Action for Happiness' article, explain the following quotations:
>   - 'epidemic of loneliness and isolation'
>   - 'turn the rising tide of excessive individualism'
>   - 'the contagious nature of happiness'
> 2. Write your own, high-quality answer to the sample exam question on page 11.

In the exam you will be expected to write about **two** non-fiction texts. Typically, of the questions you will be expected to answer, one or two of them will focus on the first text and one or two will focus on the second text. At least one question will ask you to write about both texts.

Read the web article, below, entitled 'Have a Grumpy New Year Everyone'.

The Weekly Gripe

| New Gripes | Submit Gripe | Gripe List | Contact Us |

Have a Grumpy New Year Everyone

If Christmas isn't bad enough, what about New Year? What's all that about? I've just got shot of Aunt Mildred (thank goodness) and I've sold that awful celebrity fitness DVD online. Then, just as I've started to restore my sanity once again, which is difficult after a week-long diet of dry turkey sandwiches, I have to put up with more forced jollity come New Year's Eve!

What's so special about New Year anyway? If this year was truly terrible, as it has been for a lot of people, why on earth do we want to celebrate the coming in of what is likely to be another equally disastrous year ahead of us? It's not as if turning my new Christmas calendar to January 1st will magically turn my life around – far from it. Quite apart from all of those enormous credit card bills to pay, all we have to look forward to in January 2011 is a 3% VAT hike on consumer goods; higher travel fares (yet again); filling in that dreadful self-assessment tax return and more government warnings about what a tough year we've got ahead of us. A new year also likely to manifest in hiked gas and electricity bills, heavier shopping bills, petrol price rises, falling FTSE share prices, more job losses and more news reports of MPs corruptions and scandals. The list goes on...

Some cause for celebration, that is! So far from wanting to make an idiot of myself holding hands with complete strangers in the street, singing Auld Lang Syne, I'm tempted to down a bottle of toilet bleach instead, or what is far more attractive, grab my passport and bog off to pastures new in order to escape the whole sorry saga in warmer, sunnier climates.

Oh! I forgot; the planes aren't taking off from any UK airports because a snow flake fell on a runway somewhere and, besides, I can't get to the airport in the first place because the tube workers are on strike.

So where does that leave me? Scanning the supermarket shelves to see if the price of toilet bleach has gone up and then finding out I can't pay for it because I've maxed out on my credit card? I guess I'll have to swig that left-over bottle of Christmas Champagne after all. A Grumpy New Year to you all.

Bel Grant

Read the following sample exam question. Work through the activities in the orange box, below, before writing a response to the question.

Now look at 'The Weekly Gripe: Have a Grumpy New Year Everyone'.

3. What impressions do you get of the writer of this article? Refer closely to the text in your answer.   [10]

→ CHALLENGE

1. Think of words and phrases that reveal the writer's essential personality and behaviour.
2. Discuss whether the writer's sarcasm actually includes some worthwhile social comment and criticism.
3. Discuss any points in the article that are possibly quite amusing and even witty.
4. Now construct an answer to the exam question above. Use the **Upgrade** panel, below, to check what you need to do to achieve the top grades.

Upgrade

A* ↑	answers should show a complete understanding of the text, combining specific, well-selected detail with a confident overview.
A ↑	answers should show a complete understanding of the text, exploring the text in detail and making valid comments and inferences.
B	answers should show a good understanding of the text, making valid comments and inferences.

Improving your comparative writing

The next practice exam question requires you to look back at both the 'Action for Happiness' article on page 10 and 'Weekly Gripe: Have a Grumpy New Year Everyone' on page 13.

This question tests the ability to collate from different sources and make comparisons and cross-references. It also tests the ability to develop and sustain interpretations of writers' ideas and perspectives.

→ **CHALLENGE**

Work with a partner to write a balanced and efficient answer to the following task. Follow the guidance, on this page and on the next page, to plan your argument before you write.

> **To answer the next question, you will need to consider both the newspaper report and the web article.**
>
> 4. Compare and contrast what Alexandra Topping and Bel Grant say about happiness.
>
>   Organize your answer into three paragraphs using the following headings:
>   *   material things;
>   *   people and relationships;
>   *   well-being.   [10]

Organizing your answer

There are two texts, three bullet points and ten marks – think in terms of one or two thoughtful, balanced sentences per bullet point. Each sentence should attempt to make a point about each of the texts.

How <u>not</u> to do it:

> *Both texts are very different because 'Action for Happiness' talks about happiness whereas the other text is about someone who is really grumpy and both writers are very different because one is really happy and the other is really grumpy. Also, when I read the first text I really liked it as it had a lot of happy language in it, but when I read the other one I really felt angry about the writer's attitude...*

A better approach:

> *The 'Action for Happiness' article talks about consumerism as also expressed in the second article but on the whole reacts to it differently. The author of 'Have a Grumpy New Year Everyone' wants to escape alone but the 'Action for Happiness' article is about people who want to bring 'happiness' to all to combat "an epidemic of loneliness and isolation...".*

The second example response is much better than the first; however, there is still room for improvement. The second response still lacks a little confidence. Try the following:

Bullet point 1: material things

If necessary, restrict yourself to one statement about the views presented in the newspaper report. Then, move on to a thoughtful sentence about the second text. Don't go back to simple, superficial points. Build on the previous answers. Is there a link between the two texts? Different, yet similar?

Bullet point 2: people and relationships

Some easy pickings here! Both texts have a lot to say about human beings and how they relate to each other, but also contrast in terms of language and style. State the obvious first – clearly, but carefully. Avoid 'happy – grumpy, grumpy – happy'! Try to aim for two balanced sentences at least.

Bullet point 3: well-being

What does each text say, overall, about the idea of 'well-being'? This section is likely to build on points in the first and second part of your answer.

You should also include a personal response. What is your overall reaction to the texts? Your response does not have to be extensive, but it is best if it's measured, showing some understanding of text-type and purpose. It needs to consist of a linked sentence or two, in this case, perhaps with some hint of irony. A totally miserable answer will probably say more about you than the texts!

→ CHALLENGE

1. Once you have chosen the main points of your argument, write a response to the comparative question on page 15.
2. Swap your answer with an answer from another pair and use the **Upgrade** panel, below, to grade the piece of work.
3. Put together a paragraph of feedback to justify the mark you have awarded, highlighting what worked well and what could be improved.

Upgrade

A* ↑	answers should be coherent, organized and insightful, ranging confidently across both texts.
A ↑	answers make valid comments and inferences based on a thorough and organized selection of appropriate detail from both texts.
B	answers show the ability to cross-reference in an organized way.

Key words

Persuasive techniques – Methods used by the writer to persuade, but also to tempt, convince, encourage etc. When identifying and writing about persuasive techniques, remember that the 'how' and the 'what' are closely linked. Look at what a writer says as well as how. The 'how' might be strong or it might be subtle; it might be friendly, and supportive, or it might play on other emotions.

Key words

Attitude – The writer's thoughts and feelings about the subject matter of the text. The writer's attitude may be direct and obvious or it may be mixed or subtle.

Approaching the exam

Question types

Expect some questions to require a personal response and especially your view on what the writer is up to. Expect other questions to ask you to search and find, to identify writers' attitudes and to write about **persuasive techniques**. At least one question will require you to compare texts.

Search and find questions

It may be possible to find enough points to accumulate a high mark, but a haphazard list will fall short. Clearly, good selection is important. Too many candidates think a question like this one is all about quoting and, worse still, explaining the quotations. Make a point and move on. An A* answer will organize the 'arguments' confidently. This is not meant to be a difficult question!

Questions about persuasive techniques

Get an overall angle for your answer by identifying the purpose of the text. This type of question may include bullet points, which will remind you to pick out ideas, presentational features, and words and phrases. The best answers will do this with well-reasoned authority, combining all of these elements into a coherent argument.

Questions about the writer's attitude

This type of question will always require some reasoning and explanation in order to convey your understanding of the writer's **attitude**. Answers may include key words from the text, however, the best candidates will also be able to use their own words to unravel and reorganize the text skilfully, laying bare the real intentions and attitudes behind the text.

Comparison questions

Balance and organization are the basis for success in the comparison question. You will sometimes be required to make a choice and then, in a reasonably balanced way, to justify the choice. This may require judgement on the qualities of persuasion in the texts or the viewpoints expressed by the writers. Read the exact wording of the question closely. As with all these questions, remember to step back, if only for a moment or two, to think about the direction of your response before you write.

Final word

What makes a good response to non-fiction texts?

Consistency is a key attribute. Your answers should be of roughly equal length, built upon a roughly equal allocation of time. It is worth reminding you that this is a test of reading and understanding – so teasing out the meaning thoughtfully and writing with considered authority is better than simply bashing out a long response.

Further task

You will have **one hour** in your exam to write answers to all questions. The exam paper will include two texts of roughly equal length.

Complete the following questions as if you were sitting them in the exam. You should aim to spread your time evenly between questions.

Once you have completed an answer for each question, use the **Upgrade** assessment criteria on page 21 to grade your work. Use the criteria to determine what you need to do to improve and write down three changes that could help you to boost your answer into the next grade band, or allow you to secure a stronger A*.

Read the 'Class, atten-shun' newspaper report.

1. What are the arguments in favour of ex-soldiers becoming teachers, according to the report?   [10]

2. How does the report try to influence your thoughts and feelings about ex-soldiers in schools?   [10]
   You should consider:
   • content
   • layout
   • language.

Now look at the opinion column entitled 'Should more ex-soldiers become teachers?'

3. How does Francis Gilbert try to persuade you that the idea of ex-soldiers becoming teachers is not a good one? Remember to look at what is written and how it is written.   [10]

To answer the next question, you will need to consider both the newspaper report and the opinion column.

4. Which of the texts is more effective in persuading you, and why?   [10]

Class, atten-shun! How ex-soldiers could be deployed as teachers

By Laura Clark

Friday, 15 February 2008

Swapping war zones for classrooms: Ex-soldiers could be deployed as teachers

Hundreds of former soldiers would re-train as teachers under proposals for a crackdown on violence and truancy in inner-city schools. Ex-servicemen including retired sergeant majors would be drafted in to bring a taste of military discipline to children as young as five.

Some 250 already act as mentors to disaffected teenagers in schools, teaching them skills such as first aid and map-reading. But a report out today – written by a former soldier – calls on the Government to expand the scheme and train hundreds a year as teachers.

Tom Burkard said a similar programme in the U.S. had proved an "outstanding success". Ex-servicemen could have a "profound effect" in UK schools where 220 teachers a year are injured in assaults which require at least three days off work.

His proposal was backed by the former Chief of the Defence staff, Lord Guthrie of Craigiebank, who said that it could offer an antidote to problems of youth knife crime, drugs and violence.

"This will not, of course, solve all the problems of the inner city, but it will help," he said. "It will provide youths with role models who understand discipline and self-restraint at the time in their lives when they need it most."

The Troops for Teachers programme – known as T3 – was set up in the aftermath of the 1991 Gulf War when U.S. forces were cutting numbers.

In a report published by the Centre for Policy Studies think-tank, Mr Burkard said the ex-military personnel had proved to be "excellent teachers" who had exerted "a profound effect on discipline and learning" in their schools.

Swapping war zones for classrooms: ex-soldiers could be deployed as teachers

"This is not merely because ex-servicemen are sure of their own moral authority," his report said. "They are not intimidated by adrenaline-fuelled adolescents: they have, unlike most teachers, been there before. Their job is to inspire and train raw recruits, and transform them into men and women capable of doing dangerous jobs."

Many pupils – particularly boys – tended to respect the former soldiers for succeeding in a "macho" profession."Whether we like it or not, children from more deprived neighbourhoods often respond to raw physical power," the report added.

Mr Burkard, who was a corporal in the Royal Pioneer Corps, said the programme would "improve discipline in both primary and secondary schools".

The programme would be open to former sailors and airmen as well as soldiers. They could be re-trained at a new college funded by the Department for Children, Schools and Families but administered by the Ministry of Defence.

Should more ex-soldiers become teachers?

NO: Francis Gilbert, teacher

Wednesday, 24 November 2010

The government has recently suggested that we put more ex-soldiers in the classroom by encouraging them to re-train as teachers. The subtext of these plans is that our classrooms are so out of control that drastic military action is called for; we need more of a 'boot camp' mentality in our schools.

First, let's make it clear that any notion that our schools are in such uproar that we need military intervention is false; Ofsted judges seven out of ten of them to be 'good' or 'outstanding', with behaviour in the vast majority of them being rated 'good'. You only have to log onto the Local Schools Network, a website I co-founded with some parents, to read countless stories of well-disciplined local state schools.

The education white paper contains proposals to encourage former members of the armed forces to become teachers.

Second, as a teacher who has taught for 20 years in various comprehensives, I have some major concerns about 'militarizing' our classrooms. At a previous school, I observed an ex-soldier really struggle to cope with the demands of teaching in a mixed comprehensive. He had gone into the classroom expecting all his students to obey his every word. When they didn't, he would bark at them in a sergeant-majorish way, putting his face right into theirs, spraying spit and fury over their heads. The more timid pupils would cower and simper, often bursting into tears, while the hardened ones would smirk and laugh at him, some even swearing at him, stoking even more anger.

Even though he shouldn't have been so aggressive, he couldn't help himself. He told me that the privates did not often step out of line, and if they did, they suffered greatly; the army has punitive sanctions that you can't apply in schools. "We had to train them up to be prepared to die at our command," he said. "You simply couldn't allow them to think for themselves." I feel this comment, more than any other, highlights a central problem with putting demobbed soldiers in our classrooms: in the military, independent thought can be fatal, whereas in schools, it's absolutely crucial.

The truth is that this is a deeply nostalgic policy, harking back to the two previous wars of the last century when demobbed soldiers entered our classrooms in their droves. But they were very different times; only a tiny fraction of the school population went to university and corporal punishment was rife. Times have moved on, but sadly these ideas have not.

Use the marking criteria below to assess your answers to the practice task on page 18. Work out what you could improve in order to boost your answer into the next grade band.

1. Are all of your answers well focused and thorough?
2. Have you understood and communicated with confidence the attitude and intentions of the writer(s)?
3. In your answers, have you achieved, consistently, a balance of insightful detail and secure overview?
4. In your answer to the question about persuasive techniques, are you able to integrate your comments convincingly into your argument?
5. In your answer to the comparison question, are you able to make coherent and perceptive points on both texts and organize your answer effectively.

A*

1. Do all of your answers explore the text(s) in detail and make sustainable comments?
2. Do you have a good sense of the overview of each of the texts?
3. Are you comfortable in your understanding of the attitude of the writer in each text?
4. In your answer to the question on persuasive techniques, are you able to identify key features and link them confidently to the specific meaning of the text(s)?
5. In your answer to the comparison question, do you show an organized grasp of both texts, making key points coherently?

A

1. Have you answered the questions with consistent length?
2. Have you focused on the key words of all the questions?
3. Have you built answers based on sensible use of your own words as well as quotation?
4. In your answer to the question about persuasive techniques, do you make points that reveal your understanding of the intentions of the writer(s)?
5. In your answer to the comparison question, are you able to make cross-references in an organized way?

B

Aim for A

- the essay will offer a confident, fluent and fairly thorough response to the chosen literary text
- the essay will show a good balance of overview and detail
- the essay will give a purposeful response to the task.

Aim for A*

- the essay will be well structured with a clear thematic thread that runs cohesively through the whole piece of writing
- the essay will be tightly argued, with some individuality and style
- the essay will show contextual understanding that is well judged and well integrated into the piece of writing as a whole.

Key words

Close reading – The study of a writer's language; this means focusing on a small part of a text, maybe an extract of a chapter or a scene, and looking in detail at how the writer uses particular words.

The benefit of close reading is that it helps you to achieve a deep engagement with the text. In terms of your essay for the Controlled Assessment, close reading provides some of the evidence for building a case, and stating an argument in answer to a question.

Studying an extended literary text

For GCSE English Language you have to read an extended literary text (a novel or a play) and write an essay in response to a question about it. You may be selective in your coverage of your text but your work should be informed by knowledge of the text as a whole. The word limit guidance for your essay is **approximately 800 to 1000 words**. The text must either be a Shakespeare play or one chosen from the list of texts set by the exam board.

To be successful in this part of the course, you need to take on the commitment of reading and studying your text in full, then writing a high-quality essay on it. You need to make the most of all classroom teaching about the text, while asserting your independence as a student with potential to study literature beyond GCSE.

You need to be confident in forming your own opinions about your text. Write your essay purposefully, answering the question as set and using your notes intelligently as prompts.

THE ASSESSMENT

GCSE English Language Unit 3 Section A

This unit is assessed by Controlled Assessment and you will have a total of **two hours** to write your response. This may take place across one or more writing sessions. You will be given the essay question, on the novel or play you are studying, in advance of the writing stage, enabling you to read your text and study it in relation to the task.

You may also take one **A4 page** of your own notes into the final assessment with you. This is optional and any notes that you do take in must be handed in with your essay. Your notes must not contain a draft of any part of your response.

→ CHALLENGE

Discuss: What do you think the study of literature adds to your wider education and how might it be important to your life in general?

Task types

- With high grades in mind, you must expect to answer a question that focuses on the writer's <u>skills</u> and <u>ideas</u>.
- Your appreciation of the writer's <u>skills</u> will be conveyed by your **close reading** and response to the way language is used in selected parts of the text.
- Your understanding of the writer's <u>ideas</u> will be conveyed by your wider reading and response to the whole text.
- Your essay will also be judged in terms of its clarity and **coherence** and this is where you have a genuine opportunity to show your high-level skills in reading and understanding.

Key words

Coherence – To structure your essay effectively so that your argument progresses convincingly from start to finish. To achieve this you need to build your writing through sentences, which accumulate into developed paragraphs. You also need to link points in order to build your argument, revealing your interpretation and understanding.

The task below is an example of the type of essay you might be asked to write for your assessment.

> Examine how your chosen novelist or playwright uses language to present a particular character or theme. Refer closely to the text in your answer.

The example tasks below show how this question can be adapted to relate to the exact text that you are studying.

> _Examine how Shakespeare presents the character of Tybalt in Romeo & Juliet. Consider what is written and how it is written in your answer._

> _Examine how Harper Lee presents the character of Dill in To Kill a Mockingbird. Consider what is written and how it is written in your answer._

→ CHALLENGE

Look at the example tasks above. With a partner, discuss what these tasks are asking students to write about. What key things should students do, when writing their response, to ensure they produce a good answer?

Reading your text

Because this unit is assessed by Controlled Assessment, you will know what the task is well before writing your final response. This means that you will have time in lessons to study your text and gather ideas and evidence that will help you to write your essay.

1. Read and enjoy the text.
2. Think and talk about the text in class.
3. Make notes on the task.
4. Identify what your overall position is in response to the task and identify useful evidence to support your point of view.
5. Answer the question.

Writing the essay

The following questions are commonly asked by students when planning and writing extended essays. Read the advice and complete the activities that follow.

How do I start?

Use the question to help you start and try to make at least one point in your first sentence. Don't waste words on a general introduction to your text or the writer's biographical details. It is fine to echo the question, but only if you have something to say. Straightforward repetition of the task is pointless and will not gain you any marks.

By the end of the first paragraph you should be well into the flow of your argument and moving at pace. Wherever you are in an essay – beginning, middle or end – you should be writing sentences that make points, earn you credit and move the essay forward.

→ CHALLENGE

Read the opening paragraph from a student essay below. With a partner, discuss what this student could do to improve the introductory paragraph. This opening was written in response to the following task:

Examine how Shakespeare presents the character of Tybalt in *Romeo & Juliet*.

In this essay I am going to focus on how Shakespeare presents the character of Tybalt in Romeo and Juliet. The play tells the tragic story of two families, the Montagues and the Capulets who are mortal enemies and how at every chance they get they threaten each other, which often leads to violence. Tybalt is an important part of this because he is Juliet's cousin and Shakespeare shows through what happens early on in the play that he is a leading figure when it comes to causing trouble with the Montagues. He threatens Benvolio in Act 1 Scene 1, "I hate hell, all Montagues and thee" before starting to fight with him. This suggests that Tybalt likes violence and, unlike Benvolio, who tries to calm the violence, he seems to enjoy the conflict.

How do I select the parts of the text that I want to discuss?

The question might actually tell you which part of the text to focus on, but you will still be expected to show your understanding of the whole text. You can achieve this by **cross-referencing** points from different parts of the text and also by using your knowledge of what happens at the end to reflect on the ultimate significance of the character or theme you are writing about.

Key words

Cross-reference – A cross-reference is a point made about the text, that links with (or refers across to) something that happens elsewhere in the text.

You need to be able to choose the parts of the text that relate to your task; you also need to be able to cross-reference nimbly, moving from one part of the text to another.

Read the following practice essay questions:

> How does the author explore the theme of trust in the text that you are studying?

> How does the author challenge ideals of money and wealth in the text you are studying?

> What is the significance of the setting in the text that you are studying?

→ CHALLENGE

Select one of the essay questions and think about it in relation to the text you are studying. Work through the tasks below to help you decide which parts of the text you would focus on if writing a response to your chosen essay question.

1. Identify **two** parts of the text that would be particularly relevant to answering the question. These should be parts of the text that you would focus on in some detail in your essay.
2. Choose **three** other minor events in text that you might mention to support your argument but would not need to write about in lots of detail.
3. What does the ending of the text reveal in relation to the topic you are focusing on? Would this add anything to your answer?

Avoid

Do not write a response that is an extended outpouring of your notes, without shape or direction. To reach the highest marks your essay needs to have structure and a clear line of argument.

How do I prepare my A4 page of notes?

No doubt many students will try to pack every last detail onto their sheet of notes, but the danger is that when they come to write their essays, they will not be able to see the wood for the trees.

Keep your notes fairly sparse if you can, so that when you come to write you can think with a clear head. You are not supposed to have a full essay plan or a draft on your page of notes.

The best approach is just to be honest about your efforts, and use your notes sensibly. It is important that your notes are your own and contain your own ideas.

How should I use quotation?

There is no doubt that the use of quotation is a big issue in essay writing, and it probably dominates too much as a talking-point. It is particularly difficult to generalize, but assuming you are writing an essay in a 'closed-book' situation (i.e. without access to the book), you should use quotations from memory or your notes only where they fit usefully into your essay.

Short quotations mostly work better than long ones, because they can be integrated into your commentary. Longer quotations tend to be used too often where students are providing more text than they need to illustrate a point. This slows the flow of an essay down and can actually make it more difficult for you to demonstrate the kind of critical depth you need to achieve the higher grades.

At the top level, you need to show that you are sensitive to the subtle meanings of language. You need to be able to use evidence to make **inferences**.

Do not allow yourself to be a one-trick pony with P.E.E. ('point, evidence, explanation'); useful though this is as a starting principle, just think how your essay is likely to read if you use this approach throughout. To impress at the top end, you need to be more dynamic in your analysis, using the examples and explanations you need to put your points across and to develop your argument.

→ CHALLENGE

How would you rate your own skills in terms of using evidence from texts? What could you do differently to improve your writing?

Key words

Inference – To 'read between the lines', beyond the literal meaning of the text. Not every inference shows a sound understanding, however. Be cautious and sensitive and do not jump to conclusions. Inferences can be clumsy or just plain wrong. Well-considered inferences can, however, be a sure mark of quality reading and understanding.

Read the extract from a student answer, below. What is effective about this student's use of quotation? Use the **Upgrade** panel to grade this response.

The well-known opening sentence of *Pride and Prejudice* gives the reader a very clear message as to what the story is to be about. It tells the reader that the story is related to the theme of marriage, as "a single man in possession of good fortune, must be in want of a wife". This immediately sets the scene that a rich man is looking for a woman to marry. However, in this sentence, love (nowadays, probably the most key aspect of a marriage) is not even mentioned, and nor is it in the next few paragraphs. Austen is portraying that the sole reason a woman would want to marry this man, is because he in "possession of a good fortune". Austen is also mocking the society of that era, as she says that this perception of marriage "is a truth universally acknowledged". She is saying that this idea of marrying a man for his money, is typical of society in that era, and is possibly considered the 'right' way of deciding whom to marry. This whole philosophy is what the book is based on, and is shown quite clearly through the marriage of Mr and Mrs Bennett.

Upgrade

A* ↑	The student is able to identify and locate revealing details from across the text and is able to use this evidence to form part of a cohesive argument. The student is also able to employ techniques such as paraphrasing, and using long and short quotations to best suit the flow of the argument.
A ↑	The student is able to select the best evidence from the text to support points in the essay and is able to offer detailed analysis where relevant. The student is also able to use long and short quotations as appropriate.
B	The student supports points with well-selected and relevant evidence from the text. The student is able to build quotations into the response effectively.

Practise your close reading skills by exploring the extract from *Pride and Prejudice* on the next page. In the extract, Austen pursues the theme of marriage through a conversation between Elizabeth Bennet and Charlotte Lucas. Read the passage and then write a paragraph in response to the following task:

Explain carefully how and why Charlotte justifies her decision to marry Mr Collins.

Pride and Prejudice

"Engaged to Mr. Collins! my dear Charlotte, – impossible!"

..."I see what you are feeling," replied Charlotte, –"you must be surprised, very much surprised, –so lately as Mr. Collins was wishing to marry you. But when you have had time to think it all over, I hope you will be satisfied with what I have done. I am not romantic, you know. I never was. I ask only a comfortable home; and considering Mr. Collins's character, connections, and situation in life, I am convinced that my chance of happiness with him is as fair as most people can boast on entering the marriage state."

Key words

Line of argument – A line of argument in an essay is the string of connections, paragraph by paragraph, that help to build an answer to the question.

It is not about falling out with yourself or getting yourself tied in knots of contradiction! Remember, also, that your argument will be won through the quality of your reasoning rather than through strength of feeling.

How do I develop my argument?

Be true to the question or task from start to finish. Make sure you have an overview of the likely end-product before you begin writing your answer. A limit of 800 to 1000 words is between three and five pages of writing. Each page will probably have two or three paragraphs and each paragraph should reinforce a connection with the question, explicitly or implicitly. Take care to maintain a **line of argument** throughout your answer. It is a challenge, but not one that you have to resolve perfectly.

When making points, your comments should be succinct and clear. Not casual opinions, but ones which reflect close reading and a balanced knowledge of the text as a whole.

How do I end my essay?

Conclusions can give as much heartache as openings. Writing in a Controlled Assessment may seem less daunting than the prospect of scribbling down your final paragraph in an exam, but it probably will not seem that way when you are in the thick of the action!

Try to keep something back for the last paragraph, whether it is a key word, a phrase, or a comment. You should be trying to find a fresh, strong way of wrapping it up. Probably the most important thing, though, is to have managed your time and to have organized your coverage of the text successfully, so that you do not end the two hours with an unfinished sentence.

Read the conclusions below from two student essays on *Pride and Prejudice*. Both were written in response to the same task:

> How does Jane Austen explore the theme of marriage in *Pride and Prejudice*?

...And this is what I believe Austen is trying to tell us throughout this book, that marriage should be based upon love and have that as a foundation for a relationship. Wealth and status will not guarantee one's happiness, and will almost certainly end in a bitter marriage that will not work. So the reader is left with the advice here, and is left knowing the consequence of wrong decisions, so that they may choose themselves somebody to marry whom they truly love.

...To summarize what has been said, it is clear through 'Pride and Prejudice' that Austen wants to explore the variation in marriages and how different reasons for marrying somebody, influence the relationship of the married couple. The story also shows the reader that marrying somebody that he or she truly loves will be a more successful and fulfilling marriage. Basing a marriage upon love is the start of a prosperous relationship, but on the contrary, marrying somebody for wealth, title or because someone is forcing one to, will eventually break down. The story shows this through exemplifying the marriages of Mr and Mrs Bennet, Mr Collins and Charlotte and Mr Darcy and Elizabeth.

→ CHALLENGE

Discuss the strengths and weaknesses of the example conclusions above. Which conclusion is most effective in your opinion? Be prepared to justify your answer.

Giving a personal response

When responding to literary texts at a high level, you need to be prepared to make up your own mind about what is significant and what is worth writing about. You need to pay close attention to the task, but you also need to find your own way of responding to it, informed by <u>your</u> opinions and <u>your</u> personal interest in the text.

When writing an A*-grade response, including a **personal response** does not mean stating whether you like or dislike a text; it means engaging with the text on an individual level. You need to make the leap when it comes to forming judgements about the text, building confidence in what you say through well-selected evidence.

Key words

Personal response – An honest reaction to the text by the reader, with some justification or reasoning.

At a high level, there will be clear independence of thought and expression.

Read the extract, below, from *Anita and Me* by Meera Syal. The novel tells the story of a young girl, Meena, growing up in the West Midlands during the late 1970s. The extract refers to an incident in which Meena, the narrator, steals from the local shopkeeper and then has to face her father.

Anita and Me

My humiliation had been compounded by the fact that mama was an infants' teacher in the adjoining school; we were separated by a mere strip of playground, and I knew it would only be a matter of time before she got to hear of my behaviour. I knew I should tell papa everything now, Confess said the Lord and Ye Shall Be Saved. Papa's expression made me wonder if this only ever worked with English people, but I had to say something because if we entered Mr Ormerod's shop, my crime would become public shame as opposed to personal failure and that, I knew, was something papa hated more than anything.

Somewhere a front door slammed shut. It seemed to reverberate along the terrace, houses nudging each other to wake up and listen in on us, net curtains and scalloped lace drapes all a-flutter now.

Everyone must have been watching, they always did, what else was there to do?

'Right then. We'll ask Mr Ormerod what happened.'

Papa pushed open the door of the shop, the brass bell perched on its top rang jauntily. Its clapper looked like a quivering tonsil in a golden throat and it vibrated to the beat of my heart.

'I was lying,' I said in a whisper.

Papa's face sagged, he looked down and then up at me, disappointment dimming his eyes. He let go of my hand and walked back towards our house without looking back.

→ CHALLENGE

What are your thoughts and feelings about the extract? Respond to the question with a paragraph of sound, confident writing.

→ **CHALLENGE**

Work with a partner to mark your response to the extract from *Anita and Me* on the previous page. First, swap your work with your partner. What is your overall impression of the response? Does it include evidence of thought and reasoning?

Use the **Upgrade** panel below to help you feed back to your partner on what he or she has done well and to provide focus points for future essay writing.

Upgrade

A* ↑

Achieved:
- ✓ Personal response shows engagement and reasoning.
- ✓ Views are persuasive and convincing with well-selected evidence.
- ✓ Comments on style are allied to meaning.

Focus on:
- Keeping your points fresh and flowing in a longer essay.
- Balancing detailed analysis with points about the wider text.
- Making connections between characters or between different parts of the text.

A ↑

Achieved:
- ✓ Gives sensible opinions.
- ✓ Provides convincing evidence.
- ✓ Comments on style are rational and developed.

Focus on:
- Engaging with the text on a personal level, trusting your instincts.
- Selecting pertinent evidence to support points and build your argument.
- Integrating comments on stylistic features into your wider argument.

B

Achieved:
- ✓ Gives opinions that are clearly expressed.
- ✓ Supports points with evidence from the text.
- ✓ Makes sensible comments about stylistic features.

Focus on:
- Ensuring opinions are founded on knowledge of the text.
- Being selective with evidence – choose the best examples to support your argument.
- Avoiding formulaic analysis.

Exploring the writer's intentions

If you are aiming for the top grades, you need to get in the real world! This means, that whilst the the fictional events and characters of your text will certainly make up a large part of what you write about in your essay, you also need to be very aware of the <u>role of the writer</u>.

Remember that the text you are studying is not a window into another universe; it is a piece of literature, created and crafted by another human being. Just like any artist, writers have to make decisions about how to shape their work before they create it. Try to open your mind to the possible intentions behind these decisions and be sensitive to the kind of messages or emotions the writer is trying to convey to the reader.

If you can identify what a writer is trying to do, then it makes sense to comment on how he or she is attempting to achieve it. If you are skilful in how you express this, you can combine this with a personal response.

> **➔ CHALLENGE**
>
> Look at the opening page of the text you are studying, or choose another extract that you find particularly striking. Explain to a partner what you believe the writer is trying to achieve in the extract; what techniques he or she uses and what impact it has on you. How does this compare to your wider understanding of the novel?

Demonstrating high-level skills

The following student response is based on the novel *Silas Marner* by George Eliot. Silas is a miserly weaver and social outcast who, having obsessed over a pot of gold for much of his life, discovers one day that it has been stolen.

Read the response to the essay question below and the examiner comments that show why this essay achieved top marks.

> How does Silas Marner's character change and develop in the novel?

The sentence suggests a cautious opening, but the rest of the paragraph is committed to a particular interpretation. This angle has been well considered and is carried through the essay as a whole.

In this paragraph, there is consistent evidence of high-level skills in reading and writing; the ability to integrate quotations, to cross-reference details and to use evidence to support opinions subtly, with personal response ever-present. It is confident writing that is not laboured or over-detailed.

The way that Silas Marner changes in the book is linked to how other characters treat him. The author uses a narrator who is separate from the action, allowing us, as readers, to see what is true and what is simply superstition about the man whose "dreadful stare could dart cramp". Right from the beginning, Eliot tells us that Silas' previous life was normal, showing the reader that it was others affecting his reputation that led to him losing his faith.

This continues when he moves to Raveloe, and because he does not attend church, or "drink a pint at The Rainbow" he is treated as an odd character. This combined with the weaver's unexplained fits, which are believed to be "visitations of Satan", adds to the villager's view of him as strange, and leads to the isolation of Silas. The author shows us that this view of Silas is unfair when he tries to help ill Sally Oates. We, as readers, can now see that he is not evil, and his separation from the rest of the villagers is most likely because of his distrust and lack of faith. However the good deed backfires when the community believes Silas can heal others. With Silas' refusal to do so, comes bad opinion and rumours yet again of his involvement with the devil, even to the point where they think he causes illnesses rather than healing people.

All of this leads to a negative development of Silas' character; he changes to become more reclusive, and his life "narrowing and hardening" increasingly revolves around his work. He even starts to look more sinister, he is "withered and yellow" and the more time that he spends on the loom, the more bent and withered Silas becomes, until he resembles the very witch the villagers accuse him of being.

The student continues to match detail to overview. The writing has persuasive qualities and we are never in any doubt now how well the student knows the novel.

As readers we may dislike the weaver at this point in the novel: he becomes a hoarder, completely obsessed about his gold. Through the language used to describe Silas, the author shows him as greedy, slavering over his gold, even comparing the thought of his future earnings to "unborn children". This is where Silas' character is at its lowest.

Silas changes again when his gold is stolen. He becomes more miserable, but it also leads to pity and sympathy from his neighbours. The villagers believe that if he is not "cunning" enough to keep hold of his own gold, he is not cunning enough to harm others. Various women begin to bring Silas Christmas food, and attempt to convince him to come to church. Silas, however, is not used to this kindness, and does not know how to respond to it, until the appearance of Eppie.

Implicit and explicit links to the question here, as in each paragraph so far. This response is definitely answering the question as set.

It takes a dramatic event to convince the villagers of Raveloe that Silas means no harm. When Eppie wanders into Silas' life, the author is showing us Silas' kind nature. For example when Eppie cries, Silas "unconsciously uttered sounds of tenderness" to soothe her. Eppie is the replacement of Silas' lost gold, in fact he even believes she is "his own gold – brought back mysteriously", because of her blonde hair.

The student sharpens the focus effectively here by selecting a key incident.

Later on in the chapter when the rest of the villagers see the child, she clings to Silas "who had apparently won her thorough confidence" – the first person to really trust him since he moved to Raveloe. Silas offers to look after the child, saying "it's a lone thing – and I'm a lone thing", showing how Silas and Eppie are similar. Later on as Eppie grows and develops, so does the character of Silas.

The narrator shows us how before Eppie, Silas was forced to continuously weave to gather his gold, and so ignored the villagers. Eppie stops this, and as she learns about the outside world, so does he. Eppie is described "gurgling" with triumph in the "sunny mid-day" with "winged things that murmured happily" creating a much happier image than when Silas was alone weaving. Silas stops wishing for his gold, and instead begins to think of Eppie as "his treasure".

Looking back, looking forwards – from the middle of the novel. Beautifully written and organized and conveyed with a sense of enjoyment.

Eppie's childhood seems to be a time of joy, and Silas' character develops a lot in this time. He is described as "unfolding" and the reader is told how he begins to think about his past. The similarities between Eppie's growth and Silas' can also be seen in the language of these chapters. The word "articulate" is used to describe the growth of "the tones that stirred Silas' heart" in the same paragraph as describing how Eppie has learnt to speak, or articulate, and so say "Dad-dad".

Consistent focus on the question.

Here the student demonstrates the ability to move on, not to get bogged down; to mind the clock ticking and get to the final chapters.

Throughout the rest of the book Silas thinks firstly of Eppie, and in doing so is forced to socialize with the people of Raveloe. The villagers see this as a move towards normality, and so their opinions of him begin to improve. The final chapters of the novel are set 16 years later and here we see the change and development of Silas Marner complete.

The reader meets Silas after all these years leaving a church service, showing just how much he has become a part of the community. We are told that "his eyes seem to have gathered a longer vision" and he clearly loves the grown up Eppie from the way he talks to her "with the mild passive-happiness of love". Silas seems to have realized that to be accepted is a good thing, and we see this in his new habit of smoking a pipe. He has been told this may help his fits, but his real reason to do it is "a humble sort of acquiescence in what was held to be good". The narrator tells us how Silas has blended his old faith with the beliefs of the Raveloe villagers, and this proves he has removed the barriers that once stopped the other characters from getting to know him. By doing this he has become a well-respected member of the community.

The latter half of the essay skilfully echoes the happy ending and the mood of the writer, showing that the student can definitely work on the level of ideas beyond the literal.

Throughout the novel the biggest development in Silas' character is because of Eppie. Eliot shows these changes through the different things other characters say or think about him. For example Mr Snell believes at the end of the book that "when a man has deserved his good luck (meaning Silas) it was the part of his neighbours to wish him joy". Although we may be frustrated that to gain the villagers' approval Silas is smoking when he does not enjoy it, and changing his religion, we are glad he is happy.

Double whammy. Previous paragraph could have been the conclusion, but here we have a re-enforced conclusion, which helps to add impact to the ending.

The most obvious development in Silas' character is seen in the final chapters of the novel, when he finds his gold. He does not return to his greedy self, or become obsessed with counting it, instead he just uses it to travel back to Lantern Yard, and find out if his name has been cleared. He finds out that Lantern Yard has gone, along with any chance of clearing his name, but Silas is able to see past this to the "light enough to trusten by" that Eppie brought to his life. Now that he can trust again, and has neighbours who like him, Silas can be a happier character. The author finishes the tale of Silas Marner with the marriage of Eppie and Aaron, ending the book on a happier note, letting us imagine a better future for the characters.

This is an excellent example of an A* essay in response to an extended text. It leaves the reader with no doubt about the understanding, enthusiasm, experience that this student has regarding the novel. Full marks with a bit of spare; by no means a typical answer, but it does demonstrate what kind of quality is in fact achievable within the time available.

→ CHALLENGE

What do you think is the biggest strength of the essay? Consider the examiner comments. Which skills could be applied to any text and which skills depend precisely on the text you are studying?

Wider reading

The crucial thing is to make sure you read the entire text you are studying. This may mean that you have to do some extra reading in your own time, to supplement what you have time to cover in lessons.

If this is the case, take the responsibility seriously. If you have covered the whole text in lessons, consider re-reading sections in your own time. This will help you to form your own ideas about the text and to formulate the independence of analysis that is required for the top grades.

Considering that you will be balancing the commitments in other GCSE subjects as well as English, you may or may not have time to read around your set text. This is not a requirement of the assessment, and you will not be marked on how well you know other works by the same author. However, your experience and awareness will certainly increase, the more you read.

➔ CHALLENGE

To become really purposeful about your reading, start a reading diary or blog based on the text you are studying. Use the diary or blog to record your interpretations and thoughts as you progress with your reading, bringing it up to date periodically with details such as observations, key quotations and ideas in response to your task.

Final word

What makes a good critical essay?

A top-grade student will be able to able to demonstrate assuredness in both understanding and expression. He or she will often have a light touch in technical matters, with a good sense of proportion when dealing with textual detail, knowing when to pursue a point further and when to move on. A top-grade student will be interested in the world of the characters, but will also be keen to explore the writer's intentions.

Above all, remember that you are writing your essay in response to the whole text. You will need to be selective but don't ignore obvious points.

Avoid

Don't hold back. Remember: if you write it down, it may not get a tick, but if you don't write it down, it certainly won't!

Further task

In the following task to end this chapter, focus on the ending of the novel or play that you are studying and think about how this influences your understanding of the text. Use this opportunity to develop your essay writing style and to build confidence in your ability to read and form judgements.

> How does the writer use the ending of the novel or play to present his/her ideas and perspectives?

Use the marking criteria below to assess your answer to the practice task on page 36. Decide what you could improve to help push your answer into the next grade band.

1. The essay is impressive in terms of the level of understanding and the independence of expression.
2. The essay shows an intelligent level of insight and appreciation of factors affecting and influencing the meaning of the text.
3. You are able to quote succinctly and use evidence effectively to build a cohesive argument.
4. You are able to use language with precision, selecting words to convey points clearly and convincingly.

A*

1. The essay is fluent and quite cohesive.
2. You are able to analyse the text with confidence.
3. You are able to select and include succinct, relevant evidence.
4. The response shows that you can move comfortably between the detail and an overview of text.

A

1. The essay is sustained to an appropriate length.
2. Details of the text are well-employed and relevant to the task.
3. The essay is organized competently and logically.
4. The essay shows that you are able to make sensible inferences about the text.

B

Chapter 2.1   Creative Writing

Aim for A

- the writing is developed with originality and imagination
- the writing is well crafted in an appropriate form, with evident structural and stylistic features
- material is well selected and prioritized, successfully holding the reader's interest
- a wide range of appropriate, ambitious vocabulary is used to convey meaning and create effects
- paragraphs are varied in length and structure to organize detail and sustain progression
- in narrative writing, plot and characterization are effectively constructed.

Aim for A*

- the writing is developed with marked originality and imagination
- the writing is adeptly crafted in an form that is both appropriate and effective, with distinctive structural and stylistic features
- material is purposefully selected and prioritized, firmly engaging the reader's interest
- a wide range of well-judged, ambitious vocabulary is used to convey precise meaning and create specific effects
- paragraphs are varied in length and structure to skilfully control detail and progression
- in narrative writing, plot and characterization are well constructed and effectively sustained.

Key words

Structure – This refers to how you organize your writing on a sentence level and also in terms of paragraphs. How will you sequence your paragraphs? What details will you focus on first and what will you move on to next? You also need to determine how to link paragraphs, so that your sections of writing fit together effectively.

Key words

Progression – Progression is linked to structure and relates to the pace and direction of your writing. A-grade and A*-grade responses will have a strong sense of direction and will be paced to ensure the reader's interest is held throughout. Control progression using sentence structure, skilful paragraphing and a precise choice of vocabulary.

Writing creatively

Creative writing is descriptive writing and narrative writing. Skills of description and narration can be separated and worked on, but ultimately a piece of creative writing needs to have some germ of an idea that is carried through the piece of work as a whole. This demands that you think ahead, so that you know what you want to achieve before you begin.

Good writing will impress the reader in some way. To do this, you will need to think freely and be prepared to be original. The best writing cannot be achieved by abiding by a set of rules, regulations and formulas. It is equally important that you do not try to memorize creative writing.

Can writing for a qualification fit the ideals of good, creative writing? Can writing under pressure perhaps help you to improve your skills and overall quality in all of your future writing? Can you be successfully creative, imaginative, and original? The answer to all of these questions is yes.

THE ASSESSMENT

GCSE English Language Unit 3 Section B

This unit will be assessed by Controlled Assessment. You will complete **two** pieces of creative writing in **two hours**. If the time available is split into shorter sessions, you must hand in your ongoing work at the end of each session.

Your teacher may inform you of the tasks ahead of the day, but you are <u>not</u> allowed to take any notes or drafts into your final assessment.

Descriptive writing

Descriptive writing at GCSE requires focus on a person, a place or a situation. You need to visualize the scene, in detail, in your head and then re-create it on paper.

Good writing is worth reading and talking about. That means that it needs to engage the reader. You do not need a predictable list of five senses, nor an overload of similes, metaphors, adjectives and adverbs. You can engage the reader by using the best words for the occasion.

You can also demonstrate skill in the way you **structure** your writing and control its **progression**. Descriptions should concentrate largely on one scene or situation, and in GCSE terms they are not narratives, but they do need to develop with some forward momentum.

In his novel, *On the Black Hill*, Bruce Chatwin describes a rural graveyard. Read this piece of descriptive writing and think about what makes it so effective.

On the Black Hill

By the gate into Maesyfelin graveyard there is an old yew-tree whose writhing roots have set the paving slabs askew. Rows of headstones flank the path, some carved with classical lettering, some with gothic, and all of them furred with lichen. The stone is soft; and on those that face the prevailing westerlies, the letters have almost worn away. Soon, no one will read the names of the dead and the tombs themselves will crumble into the soil.

By contrast, the more recent tombs have been cut from stone as hard as the stones of the Pharoahs. Their surfaces are polished by machine. The flowers placed upon them are plastic, and their surrounds are not of gravel, but green glass chips. The newest tomb is a block of shiny black granite, one half with an inscription, the other left blank.

Now and then, a tourist who happens to stray behind the Chapel will see, seated on the edge of the slab, an old hill farmer, in corduroys and gaiters, gazing at his reflection while the clouds pass by above.

> ### → CHALLENGE
>
> In pairs, discuss the following questions. Be prepared to share your ideas with the class.
> 1. What are the qualities of Bruce Chatwin's description?
> 2. Is this type of writing down to luck?
> 3. What is 'original' writing?

Writing with style

You will have less time than perhaps Bruce Chatwin had when writing the passage above. However, you will have enough time to produce a quality piece of writing.

To give yourself the best chance, you need to be realistic about what you intend to achieve in your assessment. An A-grade piece of writing will be well crafted and will be written in an appropriate form, with clearly realized structural and stylistic features.

This means that the writer will have created something entirely believable for the reader, with some shape to it, and some thought behind it. Not a rush job.

Read the first student response on the next page and answer the questions that follow.

The pale yellow sunlight filtered through the dewy green canopy of great oak trees that enclosed the park; it tumbled over the minute particles of dust. It illuminated the individual blades of grass that occupied the large clearing.

Idle swings hung motionless, giving an occasional sway in the light breeze. The air was dry and still: a product of summer. The only thing that disturbed the frozen peace was a young girl. She was sitting in an awkward position on the end of the slide. Her red summer dress was stained with tears, the darker colour contrasting with the bow in her hair that was bleached with daylight. Her innocent eyebrows were tightly knitted together in a frown.

→ CHALLENGE

1. Which images are effective?
2. How has the student attempted to structure the description?
3. What would you write about in the next paragraph if you went on to continue the description of the park?

Now read another piece of description, written by a student in response to the same task. The writer chooses a particularly eloquent style to describe this scene. Think about how it compares with the previous piece of writing.

The bright autumn sunshine tumbled down through the red-gold leaves of the trees. Jack Frost had already kissed the grass with his silvery white lips. The calm setting at Berry Hill Rugby Football Club did not reflect the action that was taking place on its premises.

Supporting parents and coaches lined the perimeter of the pitches, shouting encouragement and offering advice. Some, less restrained adults yelled as if they were spectators at a Gladiator fight in Ancient Rome – baying for blood. But this was certainly not the Coliseum.

→ CHALLENGE

1. What features of the second piece of writing help to give it a particular 'style'?
2. How is the second piece of writing structured?
3. Use the **Upgrade** panel, below, to judge both answers and give each answer a grade from B to A*.
4. Continue the second response, by writing the next two paragraphs in the same style as the opening section.

Upgrade

A* ↑	the writing is skilfully crafted using an effective form, with distinctive structural and stylistic features.
A ↑	the writing is well-crafted in an appropriate form, with evident structural and stylistic features.
B	the writing makes good sense and is properly organized.

Writing with originality and imagination

Is it possible to enjoy writing? Here is what some students had to say:

❝*Yes, if you are writing about something that interests you.*❞

❝*No, because it demands a lot of thinking.*❞

❝*Yes, of course, it's great to let your imagination flow and your ideas flourish.*❞

❝*Yes, 'writing' is not specific and I believe everyone has a type and style of writing that they can usually enjoy.*❞

❝*Only if you write about something you believe in.*❞

➜ CHALLENGE

Read the opinions above and then discuss the following with a partner:
1. Is good writing hard work?
2. Is writing a response to a set task a fair test of creativity?
3. How could you make a response to a set task meaningful to you?

> **Key words**
>
> **Sophistication**
> – Writing with 'sophistication' means writing with control and style; using language and structure confidently to achieve specific effects.

In the context of your GCSE, achieving 'originality' does not mean that you have to come up with something entirely world-changing; it simply requires a little extra personal thought around the task.

A*-grade answers will show a great deal of sophistication when it comes to choice of content and the organization of detail within the piece of writing. When it comes to descriptive writing, **sophistication** really means writing with control and style; it means you are on top of what you are doing and you are not writing to a formula.

➜ CHALLENGE

Describe the scene at a busy tourist attraction. You could describe a theme park, a museum, a zoo or an historic site. However, you are free to use your own ideas.

Choosing the right words

You can also show sophistication through your choice of language. To produce an A-grade piece of writing, you need to be able to use a wide range of ambitious vocabulary that is both appropriate and effective. However, you do not need to swallow a dictionary! The best word is the word that fits the occasion. Obviously, if you have an extensive vocabulary, it's an advantage, but you can misfire by trying too hard.

You will not gain marks by inserting long words for the sake of it, or for including as many adjectives as you can think of. In an A* piece of writing, the reader will get the sense that each word has been chosen and positioned with skill in order to create a precise impression.

Read the student response below with comments from the examiner.

A phrase captures perfectly a social movement – watching football on TV with mates.

...On the hottest day of the year, the frozen foods department provides a cool shopping stop. An aisle, which usually prompts the turning up of collars, buttoning of coats and a chilly shudder, today allowed cool relief from the stifling heat. The freezers worked day and night to ensure that, hence the whining hum around these points.

These two general phrases show, with a tinge of exaggeration perhaps, how everyone notices the sudden climate change in this part of the store.

The drinks aisle is proving popular, not least because of the warmth, but the looming World Cup is also taking its toll and causing increasingly rapid sales of the drinks on offer. A group of four 'typical' university students push a trolley laden with drinks on promotion. They are loud and excited by what their limited budget can afford and spend no longer than they need to, making their way to the self-checkout counter. Here also, a slender lady pays for a vibrant assortment of fruit in her possession. She too is pleased with her buys, her health awareness notions stirring in delight at the five-a-day she has picked out for herself for the upcoming week.

The sense of an overload of cheap drinks, speedily filling the trolley, no time to waste. Rich description done naturally.

Nice touch, suggesting the confidence and impatience of young people.

A different, contrasting style of shopping – precision buying!

Generally, notice how few adjectives there are in the extract; how success comes with a mixture of observation and imagination.

→ CHALLENGE

1. Decide how you would rate this response in terms of use of vocabulary, using the **Upgrade** panel on the right as a guide.
2. Continue the description of the supermarket by adding two further paragraphs, selecting the best vocabulary to suit your purpose.

Upgrade

A* ↑	a wide range of well-judged, ambitious vocabulary is used to convey precise meaning and create specific effects.
A ↑	a wide range of appropriate, ambitious vocabulary is used to convey meaning and create effects.
B	a range of vocabulary is used to convey meaning clearly and to create some effects.

→ **CHALLENGE**

Describe the scene at one of the following, taking care with your choice of vocabulary:

- an amusement arcade
- an abandoned building
- an airport.

Avoid

Avoid deliberately planting metaphors and similes in your writing. Do not write to a formula!

Once you have written your response, swap it with a partner. Read your partner's response. How would you rate his or her choice of language? Complete the activities below and then give feedback to your partner.

→ **CHALLENGE**

1. Annotate your partner's piece of writing with your thoughts and comments.
2. Highlight the words and phrases that work particularly well.
3. Underline words and phrases that are less effective and suggest possible improvements or alternatives.
4. Use the **Upgrade** panel on the previous page to grade the overall use of language.

Writing with structure

The next example of descriptive writing is notable because the writer successfully combines language and structure to give the description a 'living quality'. This works primarily on a sentence level. The writer has built each sentence with precision, to control the pace of the writing and to highlight particular details.

The sun was rising over the African plains, the orange glow illuminating the landscape and breathing life into every animal and plant. Trees rustled with a warm breeze and the lake rippled under the force of it. There was movement but not a single sound disturbed the peace. Everything awoke noiselessly and gradually opened their eyes to the bright morning. There was no sound, not even a leaf caught in the wind. There was nothing. It was like the sound had been taken and had been replaced with the glorious heat of the sun. Suddenly, out of the silence a bird cheeped, a warthog grumbled, the lions purred and the whole landscape became alive and full of energy. The orange and yellow world turned brighter; colourful and vibrant birds flew from the trees, striped zebras grazed and flowers burst into bloom.

→ **CHALLENGE**

1. What techniques work well in the response above?
2. Write your own piece of descriptive writing, using language and sentence structure to create a convincing sense of movement. Choose from one of the following topics: a train journey, a passing storm, a shopping centre at closing time.

Narrative writing

When producing narrative writing at GCSE, you need to take into account the limitations of time and therefore length. Plot-driven stories (i.e. plots with endless twists of suspense and surprise) are not advised. Mature, controlled writing is your aim. Above all, focus on a credible opening and work out how you are going to end your writing before you begin.

Base your writing on experience; much of the best writing has its roots in autobiography, either directly or indirectly. Read the following extract from Bill Bryson's tales of childhood, entitled *The Life and Times of The Thunderbolt Kid*:

The Life and Times of the Thunderbolt Kid

So this is a book about not very much: about being small and getting larger slowly. One of the great myths of life is that childhood passes quickly. In fact, because time moves more slowly in Kid World – five times more slowly in a classroom on a hot afternoon, eight times more slowly on any car journey of over five miles (rising to eighty-six times more slowly when driving across Nebraska or Pennsylvania lengthwise), and so slowly during the last week before birthdays, Christmases and summer vacations as to be functionally immeasurable – it goes on for decades when measured in adult terms. It is adult life that is over in a twinkling.

The slowest place of all in my corner of the youthful firmament was the large cracked leather dental chair of Dr D.K.Brewster, our spooky, cadaverous dentist, while waiting for him to assemble his instruments and get down to business. There, time didn't move forward at all. It just hung.

Dr Brewster was the most unnerving dentist in America. He was, for one thing, about a hundred and eight years old and had more than a hint of Parkinsonism in his wobbly hands. Nothing about him inspired confidence. He was perennially surprised by the power of his own equipment. 'Whoa!' he'd say as he briefly enlivened some screaming device or other. 'You could do some damage with *that*, I bet!'

Worse still, he didn't believe in novocaine. He thought it dangerous and unproven. When Dr Brewster, humming mindlessly, drilled through rocky molar and found the pulpy mass of tender nerve within, it could make your toes burst out of your shoes.

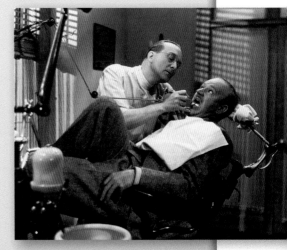

We appeared to be his only patients. I used to wonder why my father put us through this seasonal nightmare, and then I heard Dr Brewster congratulating him one day on his courageous frugality and I understood at once, for my father was the twentieth-century's cheapest man. 'There's no point in putting yourself to the danger and expense of novocaine for anything less than the whole or partial removal of a jaw,' Dr Brewster was saying.

'Absolutely,' my father agreed. Actually he said something more like 'Abmmffffmmfff,' as he had just stepped from Dr Brewster's chair and wouldn't be able to speak intelligibly for at least three days, but he nodded with feeling.

'I wish more people felt like you, Mr Bryson,' Dr Brewster added. 'That will be three dollars, please.'

→ CHALLENGE

How does Bill Bryson successfully entertain his readers in this extract?

Choosing a first- or third-person narrative

Before beginning a piece of descriptive or narrative writing, you have choices to make in terms of **form**, including whether to write from a first-person or a third-person perspective. There are advantages and disadvantages to both. However, one approach might suit your intended style and subject matter more than the other.

> ➔ **CHALLENGE**
>
> 1. Look back at the extract from *On the Black Hill* on page 40. What is particularly effective about Bruce Chatwin's choice of perspective?
> 2. Discuss the characteristics, advantages and difficulties of first-person and third-person narratives.

Engaging your reader

Engaging the reader is the purpose of all narrative writing and should therefore be a priority as you write. Bill Bryson is very successful in this respect and likewise the best responses from the Controlled Assessment will be developed with originality and imagination.

Originality comes from deciding upon a believable situation and developing it thoughtfully. Imagination is to a large extent built on experience and memory.

> ➔ **CHALLENGE**
>
> Read the following response to a task entitled 'The obsession'. Discuss with a partner:
> 1. What is effective about this piece of writing?
> 2. Does the response differ from how you might have approached the task?
> 3. What makes this piece of writing original?

Key words

Form – Style and form are closely linked and basically refer to how you have chosen to present your piece of writing. For example, have you decided to opt for a light-hearted, first-person description of people in the scene or a third-person, rather poetic portrayal of the surrounding scenery? The important thing is that the form is appropriate to your subject matter and that you are able to sustain it.

The diary of an ABBA Obsessive

Thursday December 16th

9:15 am – Am in History and have just finished test on Russia, twenty minutes before everyone else. Probably means didn't revise enough. Janna just sent note. Says, 'How's the obsession going?' Problem with Janna is, she never seems to get the message. I like to use the word 'interest', not obsession. Admittedly, it is a very strong interest. Could be worse though, could be the 'Rolling Stones' or something! Anyway, rewind. Woke up after incredible dream about you-know-who. As usual, very gorgeous. Of course, had to try on ABBA style outfit bought yesterday, all bright colours and pleated-style material. Mum thinks impractical, I think very glam. Then, had to enter real world and put on awful uniform. Bet ABBA would never have worn bottle-green! Mum asked why it takes me so long to do my hair in morning. Mum's great but does not understand teenagers! Uh-oh! Miss just asked why essay so short. Replied amazing how much info can fit into one and a half paragraphs. Miss not impressed. Think I will have to search brain cells for some dregs of knowledge to put on test paper. Have to go.

_7:00pm_ – Have just seen 'Abbamania' on TV. Makes me very annoyed. Most can't even dance like ABBA, let alone sing! I mean bands like Westlife and Steps! Actually, I quite like Steps. You get the point though. Went upstairs to play 'ABBA Gold' – real music! Next door phoned to complain about floor shaking. Oops. Must stop going so mad when practising moves to 'Dancing Queen'. Got to go, will miss ABBA documentary. Night! Frieda xxx

→ CHALLENGE

1. Write a good-humoured paragraph about another sporting or musical 'obsession', for example an Arsenal fan on match-day, fearing the worst.
2. Swap your paragraph with a partner and use the **Upgrade** panel, below, to rate your partner's work in terms of originality and imagination.

Upgrade

A* ↑	the writing is developed with marked originality and imagination. It is very believable and has obviously been well thought-out. The writer has taken an individual approach to the task.
A ↑	the writing is developed with originality and imagination. It is believable and works well overall. The writer has clearly put some personal thought into selecting and writing the content.
B	the writing has been developed with some thought and imagination. It is clear that the writer has made some clear choices before writing.

Developing a plot and characters

While your narrative writing will be marked partly in terms of how effectively you have constructed a 'plot' and 'characters', you will need to judge wisely the amount of time you have and how much you can expect to write in that time. The best strategy is to use the time you have available to produce quality writing, rather than going all-out to achieve the impossible.

A-grade answers will include a well-constructed storyline and characters. An A* answer will create and <u>sustain</u> both with skill. To achieve this, the writer will have avoided a plot with lots of twists and turns. The storyline will be simple and manageable and there will be a small number of well-realized characters.

Below are the opening and closing paragraphs of a piece of writing entitled 'The wedding'. This student has handled the demands of plot and characterization very well within the limits of the assessment. Read the response along with comments from the examiner.

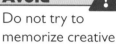

Avoid

Do not try to memorize creative writing!

Opening paragraph

Very simple, familiar statement. A short sentence with a full stop!

So here it was, the big day. Everyone had been looking forward to it, everything was ready, the tables were set, the flowers were laid out and everyone was getting ready. All they needed now was the bride...

Familiar, comfortable features in list form, then a teasing end to the short paragraph.

Closing paragraph

...They had finally found her. She was wandering through a park. She wasn't too hard to notice in her white dress that seemed to glow in the sun. As her family got closer to her she noticed them and just stared in shock. Then after a minute or two, she ran up to her mum with her tears rolling down her face. She hugged her mum and questioned herself why she wasn't at the church. Her mum took her by the hand and wiped her tears away and then looked at her and said, 'let's go get you married'. The bride just smiled as they walked back to the car.

Quite a shocking, out-of-place image, made effective by the understated voice of the narrator.

Skilful touch of the writer to bring in a single, telling piece of dialogue, mum to daughter.

The opening sets the expectations. The bride may merely be late in the best traditions of weddings, or perhaps not. The ending resolves the problem, though it may also prompt a few more questions.

➜ CHALLENGE

Decide how you might tackle the middle section of this piece of writing, given the mystery and tension of the opening and the effectiveness of the ending. What decisions would you make in terms of plot and characterization?

Controlling the pace of your narrative

Controlling the pace of your writing goes hand in hand with managing the plot and maintaining the reader's interest. Students who submit A*-grade narratives are often quite ruthless in terms of leaving things out. They do not set out to faithfully place events on record, but select the events of the narrative purposefully.

The best pieces of writing will consist of a series of deliberately placed sections, linked by association, showing inner organization and moving things on effectively.

> *"Keep up with me; you don't know what floor she's on now!" Marina exclaimed with frustration. Ruby quietly followed her older sister through the long and wide hallway of the hospital. It had been the same routine for Ruby and her sister for five months now. Ruby was a dainty twelve-year-old girl who had recently just moved into her sister's flat. Ruby and her sister got to the end of the hallway and waited for a lift to come down to the third floor. There was a distinctive smell, which wafted in the air throughout the building. Ruby resented it as it seemed to haunt her daily life...*

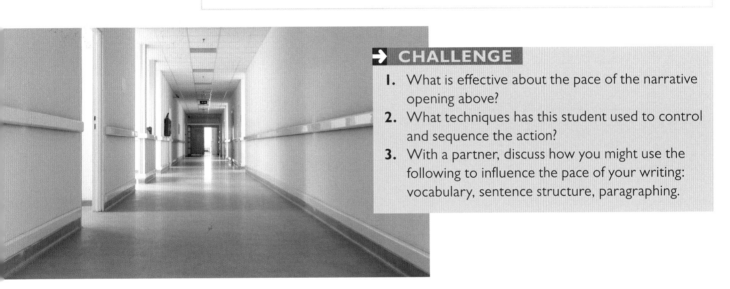

→ CHALLENGE

1. What is effective about the pace of the narrative opening above?
2. What techniques has this student used to control and sequence the action?
3. With a partner, discuss how you might use the following to influence the pace of your writing: vocabulary, sentence structure, paragraphing.

You can vary the length and structure of paragraphs to control detail and progression. Remember that variety in length of paragraphs actually comes from having a standard length of paragraph. Three or four paragraphs to a page might be the norm - then the shorter or longer paragraph might be used to create impact or intensity.

→ CHALLENGE

1. Write three further paragraphs to continue the hospital narrative above, using the length and structure of each paragraph to control the pace of the writing.
2. Write a narrative in response to one of the following titles, using a range of techniques to skilfully control the pace of the writing:
   - The biggest risk I ever took
   - A narrow escape
   - A moment in the spotlight

Using dialogue effectively

When done well, dialogue can convey convincing characters. It can also move the narrative forward and create **mood and atmosphere** in your writing. You are not writing a script for a soap opera, however, so you need to be efficient with your dialogue, successfully combining it with description and other aspects. Good, tight dialogue comes from thoughtful planning and conscious engagement with the narrative.

> She realized it was a mistake as soon as she turned the corner. Why had she agreed to see him? She owed him nothing. And yet... Oh well. No turning back now. A cold breeze lashed her face as she rounded the second corner and put herself in sight of him.
>
> "Oh God," she thought, "He looks terrible."
>
> The man had a gaunt face, coated in thick brown stubble. His cold, black eyes seemed pained and filled with loss. Conflicting feelings churned in her body. Her heart went out to him as soon as he was in sight but her mind knew better and was whispering warnings.
>
> Remember what he did to mum. This thought immediately rebuilt the walls around her heart and she approached him with a hard face.
>
> "Sarah..." His voice was raspy and quiet, cracking as though weakened through fatigue.
>
> "Hey," she said. Despite her resolve not to break, her voice still came out soft and loving.
>
> "I'm so glad you came," he rasped, "I haven't seen you in so long..."
>
> Sarah listened to a speech she had heard a number of times. It was funny how he could still make her heart ache; still give her that false hope that, one day, he would change.
>
> "Are you clean?" she suddenly interrupted.
>
> Raw shock crossed his face, followed immediately by defensiveness. He hadn't expected her to be so blunt. In fact, he hadn't expected her to be any different from the little girl who kept his secrets all those years ago.
>
> "C'mon sis, you know how hard it is to quit. I'm trying. I really am. It's just the crowd you know. They all do it so I think why not? And then all of a sudden I'm in too deep..."

→ CHALLENGE

1. What judgments does a writer have to make when creating dialogue?
2. How has the above writer fared?
3. Choose one of the tasks below and write a response to it, building effective dialogue into your writing to convey a sense of character and to infuence the overall tone and atmosphere of the piece.
   - Write about an incident which taught you the value of money.
   - Write about a time when you had to make a difficult choice.
   - Continue the following: He knew this would be his last chance.

Key words

Mood and atmosphere – Characters have moods and settings have atmosphere. This relates to the emotions that you are trying to convey in your writing. It is about choosing your language and description with skill to make these emotions clearer to the reader.

Avoid

Avoid over-writing. You do not have the time to be repetitive. Overdoing your character's emotions and overloading your description with unnecessary vocabulary is a sure way to destroy any sense of style.

Improving your writing skills

You can improve your writing skills by reading more and paying close attention to your technical accuracy. This applies to any form of writing. You need to take responsibility for this and the more attention you can give it in your own time, the better.

Can more reading improve your writing? Here is what some other students said:

> **"** *Yes, my vocabulary has certainly improved.* **"**

> **"** *Yes, it has inspired me with different styles of writing.* **"**

> **"** *I don't feel like I read enough for it to make an impact.* **"**

> **"** *No, I prefer to isolate myself from all other forms of writing in order to preserve my own personal style.* **"**

> **"** *Does reading humorous 'chick-lit' books count?* **"**

> **"** *Yes, reading gives me ideas about things I'd like to write about.* **"**

➜ CHALLENGE

Read the opinions above and then answer the following questions. Be prepared to share your views with the class.
1. Can your writing improve if you don't read much?
2. Is your writing bound to improve if you read a lot?
3. Do we read more than we think we do?

Technical accuracy

All of your descriptive and imaginative efforts will go to waste if you do not write accurately. You must consistently pay attention to technical accuracy on two fronts and try to:

- avoid careless errors
- improve your style.

In most pressurized situations, you should try to strike a balance between being ambitious and maintaining a high level of accuracy. It is understood that occasional errors will occur under pressure, but that is no excuse for failing to tackle bad habits or weaknesses that you have in your writing.

Punctuation

An A-grade piece of writing will be accurate and punctuation will be used with skill to control the writing. To achieve an A*, you need to be able to use accurate punctuation to vary pace, clarify meaning, avoid ambiguity and create deliberate effects.

If your punctuation lets you down, your sentence structure will probably also be shaky. Do not plant semi-colons and colons anywhere in your writing just to impress! Get your full-stops right, study how the comma should be used, and build carefully with the more complex items.

→ CHALLENGE

1. Write an opening paragraph of narrative writing in response to one of the following titles:
   - The dangerous game.
   - A journey to remember.
   - The local celebrity.
2. Swap your paragraph with a partner. Check your partner's use of punctuation, making corrections where required and suggesting how punctuation might be used to create effects.

Sentence structure

Top-grade pieces of writing will include a variety of sentence structures. There will be sophisticated use of simple, compound and complex sentences to achieve particular effects.

Remember that variety of sentence structure comes from being able to use a simple sentence properly. The short sentence in one form or another can be very effective. Complex sentences can be quite straightforward, so don't get in a muddle by letting your sentences run out of control. Always end a sentence before that happens. Particular effects come from controlled writing, not muddled writing.

Verb tenses

To write an A* piece of description or a narrative, you will need to have confidence with tense changes and be able to use them purposefully. Proficiency with verb tenses is more complex than simply making decisions about whether to write in the present or past. Uncertain use of things like conditionals and past participles can undermine your writing at a high level.

Read the following piece of descriptive writing, below. It is taken from *Adventure on the High Teas*, by Stuart Maconie.

Adventure on the High Teas

You can get up to British Camp (Herefordshire Beacon) in fifteen minutes from the road, and everyone does, the grannies, the aunties, the back-packers, the kids, the dogs, the courting couples. For me, though, the pass below British camp is a place of pilgrimage for reasons that are nothing to do with patriotism or antiquarian ramparts. Just by the car park is a wooden kiosk that has been there for many years and where, come rain and shine, a smiling Goth girl with multi-coloured hair and woollies will sell you a polystyrene cup of steaming tea, a bacon sandwich and the best ice cream you will ever taste in your life.

→ CHALLENGE

1. How has Stuart Maconie made effective use of tense in the extract?
2. What are modals and conditionals and how might you use them?
3. How might a change in tense be effective? Think about forms and variants of past, present and future.

Spelling

As you might expect, in an A*- or an A-grade answer, virtually all spelling, including that of complex irregular words, needs to be correct. Sound spelling is built upon good habits and thoughtful use of vocabulary. Occasional slips can be tolerated, but avoid regular errors with common words.

→ CHALLENGE

In pairs, make a list of spellings that you feel are perhaps commonly misspelt. Select five and devise a way to remember the correct spelling. Be prepared to share your ideas with the class.

Final word

What makes good creative writing?

It would be good if you avoided 'formula' writing, which is simply a set of rules designed to 'tick boxes'. If you have a good grasp of realism, you will have a good basis for description and good control over the narratives that you write. Avoid the exaggerated plot – too much information! Also, you don't need lots of characters to make your writing believable. If you can create one or two characters to dominate your narrative, the signs are promising.

Technically, when you have a comfortable control of sentence structures and punctuation, you've arrived. When your writing is complex, as intended, and not just confusing, you are matching content and skills as a proper writer. You do not need to show off with over-elaborate vocabulary and grammar – just make sure that your use of both is appropriate to the effects you want to achieve.

Further task

In your Controlled Assessment, you will have to write **one** piece of <u>descriptive writing</u> and **one** piece of <u>narrative writing</u>.

Complete the following task as if writing your response in a real Controlled Assessment. Spend no more than one hour on each piece of writing.

Once you have finished each response, use the **Upgrade** assessment criteria on the next page to grade both pieces of work. Use the criteria to determine what you need to do to improve and write down three changes that could help you to boost your answer into the next grade band, or allow you to secure a stronger A*.

---

1. Write a page of **description** on ONE of the topics listed.
   - Describe a place worth visiting.
   - Describe the scene in a shop or restaurant.

2. Choose one of the following options and write a **narrative** of two to three sides.
   - My big mistake.
   - The missing person.
   - Write about a time when you felt disappointed.

Use the marking criteria below to assess your answers to the practice task on page 54. Work out what you could improve in order to boost your answer into the next grade band.

Upgrade

Descriptive writing

1. Is your descriptive writing lively and sustained and does it keep the reader interested throughout?
2. Is it mature and perceptive?
3. Is it stylish and well-constructed and credible throughout?
4. Are the words, phrases and sentences thoughtful and varied?
5. Is your punctuation accurate and controlled?
6. Is virtually all your spelling correct and are you in control of verb tenses?

Narrative writing

1. Is your imaginative writing satisfyingly individual to you?
2. Are the plot and characters thoughtfully constructed and developed?
3. Does the narrative keep the reader's interest from beginning to end?
4. Is the narrative recognizably subtle and skilful?
5. Are the words, phrases and sentences thoughtful and varied?
6. Is your punctuation accurate and controlled?
7. Is virtually all your spelling correct and are you in control of verb tenses?

A*

Descriptive writing

1. Is the content of your descriptive writing sensible, purposeful and engaging?
2. Is your writing organized and sustained quite effectively?
3. Do your words and phrases display a range of vocabulary?
4. Are your sentences controlled, reasonably varied and effective?
5. Are your spelling and vocabulary reasonably ambitious and accurate?
6. Are you confident and deliberate about any changes of verb tenses?

Narrative writing

1. Do the subject and content of your imaginative writing have some personal input and decision-making?
2. Does your narrative have a thoughtful opening and a credible ending?
3. Are the plot and characters sensibly developed?
4. Are your sentences controlled, reasonably varied and effective?
5. Are your spelling and vocabulary reasonably ambitious and accurate?
6. Are you confident and deliberate about any changes of verb tenses?

A

Descriptive writing

1. Is your descriptive writing relevant, focused and coherent?
2. Is it organized and sustained?
3. Do the words, phrases and sentences suggest a thoughtful approach?
4. Is your punctuation reliable and controlled?
5. Is your spelling accurate?
6. Are you well in control of Standard English grammar?

Narrative writing

1. Is the content a result of some thoughtful background thinking?
2. Are your plot and characters sensible and controlled?
3. Is your writing paragraphed and the narrative generally well organized and well presented?
4. Is your punctuation reliable and controlled?
5. Is your spelling accurate?
6. Are you well in control of Standard English grammar?

B

Aim for A

- the writing shows sound understanding of the purpose and format of the task
- the writing shows strong awareness of the reader/intended audience
- content coverage is well judged and detailed
- arguments are convincing and supported by relevant detail
- a wide range of appropriate, ambitious vocabulary is used to convey meaning and create effects
- paragraphs are varied in length and structure to control progression.

Aim for A*

- the writing shows sophisticated understanding of the purpose and format of the task
- the writing shows sustained awareness of the reader/intended audience
- content coverage is well judged, detailed and pertinent
- ideas are selected and prioritized to construct a sophisticated argument
- a wide range of well-judged, ambitious vocabulary is used to convey precise meaning and create specific effects
- paragraphs are varied in length and structure to control progression with skill.

Writing Information and Ideas

Writing information and ideas is <u>transactional</u> and <u>discursive</u> writing. In modern terms, this is effectively public or private writing, created with a clear sense of purpose and audience. It is writing with a clear job to do. You will have to make a case or try to win an argument.

This kind of writing is often done to a **format**, but it is certainly not best done to a formula. The text types you might come across are article, letter, speech, leaflet, report, review and there may be others. While using the right features for the format is important, the true challenge is to be effective with both the content and organization of the writing as well as its style and technical accuracy.

> **Key words**
>
> **Format** – A particular way of organizing information and presenting it. Adopting a format means including specific visual and stylistic clues in your writing so that the reader knows what type of text it is. For example, you might use 'Yours sincerely' at the end of a letter or use sub-headings to structure a report.

THE ASSESSMENT

GCSE English Language Unit 2

This unit will be assessed by an exam lasting **one hour**. You will be required to complete **two** tasks, which will ask you to produce two pieces of transactional or discursive writing, each with a different audience and purpose. Tasks will be set with a real-world context and will specify the format required, such as a letter or article.

Transactional writing

In practice, all writing in this unit is 'transactional' – tasks that require the writer to have good awareness of 'audience' and 'purpose'. The term is easiest understood in the case of a formal letter from one person to another, involving a business transaction, but in a wider sense it could also relate to any text attempting to persuade the reader to adopt a particular point of view.

Discursive writing

Discursive writing conjures up thoughts of essays on literature or topics of general interest. However, tasks in the examination may give the writer a chance to branch out and develop considered opinions and a balance of 'information and ideas'. Discursive writing is a close relative of transactional writing.

What you should and should not do

Do

- take the full **60 minutes** and use the time evenly across both tasks.
- focus on the 'purpose and audience' for each task.
- spend time thinking and planning.

Don't

- start before you have good, crisp sentences in your head.
- spoil an overall effect with ill-considered waffle.
- make knee-jerk points using bogus quotes and statistics.

Formal and informal English

One aspect that you will need to consider is how formal or informal your writing is going to be. You probably know what both of these terms mean, but do not adopt the idea that you only have a choice of two 'modes' when you come to write.

There are varying <u>degrees of formality</u>. You may find it effective, for example, to alter the level of formality at various points. The voice (or register) is critical to the success of your argument and your ability to persuade the reader.

You must be able to write **Standard English**. To coin a phrase, Standard English should be your 'default position'. You can move from light-hearted to serious and back again within a few lines if you have the skill and sensitivity to do it. You can play around with fashionable terms, but use them knowingly. Control your words, phrases, sentences, and, above all, your punctuation.

Key words

Standard English – To write in Standard English you need to be accurate in terms of your spelling, punctuation and grammar. You also need to consider your choice of vocabulary. Generally speaking, Standard English falls roughly in the middle between the Queen's English and colloquial language.

→ CHALLENGE

Write a response to the practice exam question below, thinking carefully about your choice of tone and the level of formality.

There are several well-established programmes on TV that 'showcase' the skills and talents of the public. These range from dancing to cooking, from classical singing to novelty acts.

Imagine you have a friend or relative who has decided to audition for a talent show on television.

Write a letter to your friend or relative, giving your opinions and advice. [20]

Writing an effective opening

In the pressurized situation of an exam, writing to your full potential is not easy. More than ever, your opening is vital – if you don't position yourself correctly to make the case you want to, you can ruin your whole piece before you start. Think the situation through first.

Avoid

Don't panic. Start thoughtfully and carefully, and then build your writing from there.

The exam question will establish the format, purpose and audience for each task but you may have to make one or two imaginative decisions in order to really focus your writing. If the task asks you to write to a friend or relative, decide which friend or relative you should write to. If you are asked to write a review of a place you have visited, decide what place this will be. What line are you going to take about a controversial subject? You need to make these decisions before you start writing.

→ CHALLENGE

Discuss the following openings written by GCSE students. What sense do you get of the purpose and audience in the writing? What is each opening trying to achieve? How successful is each one?

1

A rough guide to Wigston

Wigston. Situated on the border of Leicester, slap-bang in the centre of the country, Wigston just about achieves the award for being furthest away from any vaguely 'nice' beach. Wigston. Imagine a small town, placed, or as some may say, dumped, on the top of a hill, with a scattering of shops and a few tender OAP's roaming the cozy cafes and tempting tearooms.

2

What's on in the city

The centre of Leicester has now been dominated by a shining new mass of glass and steel named The Highcross Shopping Centre. On the very first week of the centre opening its doors, my family and I decided to go and visit the heavily advertised restaurant strip, and, once there, we were drawn into Wagamama's: a modern take on ancient oriental dining. The frontage was a sleek, black colour and the inviting doors, along with the attentive staff, ushered us politely in...

3

Visit the Forest of Dean

The Forest of Dean is a hidden gem of this great country and the heartbeat of the forest is Coleford. This bustling, traditional market town offers beautiful scenery alongside historic architecture.

4

<u>Sporting blog: The trouble with relegation</u>

As a Leicester City Football fan, relegation is something I am more than familiar with. From the highs of being promoted to the big money Premier League to relegation and back down to the doom and gloom of the championship and yet worse, League One. It can cost millions when a club 'goes down', sometimes sending them into administration and eventually bust. 'Parachute payments' are given by the Football Association to relegated teams to help them keep their heads above the rising water, but in my opinion wages should be halved and the money should be kept to keep the fans happy. Surely, it should be illegal for Wayne Rooney to earn more in half a year than my and your parents earn in a lifetime? It's daylight robbery, if you ask me...

To achieve the highest grades in this part of your course you need to demonstrate a sophisticated understanding of the purpose and format of the task.

You also need to show a sustained awareness of the reader or intended audience. Your content therefore needs to be well judged, detailed, and pertinent.

→ **CHALLENGE**

Look back at the opening, above, and those on the previous page. With a partner, decide which of them are most likely to achieve an A*. Refer to the **Upgrade** panel below to help you and be prepared to explain your reasons to the class.

Upgrade

A* ↑	The text has a very clear and consistent sense of purpose. It gives the impression that it is trying to achieve a particular aim and I feel like I know where I stand as a reader.
A ↑	The text has a strong sense of purpose and this is generally upheld throughout the text. I get the impression that the text is trying to persuade me to think about the subject matter in a particular way and it is easy for me to understand what kind of reaction the writer is expecting.
B	The text is generally quite focused. However, there may be one or two points that seem a little overcomplicated or perhaps slightly off-topic. I can see what the writer is trying to do, although there may be one or two competing interests.

Making your thoughts clear

Before you start to write anything, give yourself some thinking time, so that you can deal with complex ideas by keeping your expression uncomplicated. In the exam you can scribble a sequence of thoughts on the question paper to give your writing some direction and organization.

To achieve the highest marks you need to ensure that your arguments are developed and supported by relevant detail. You also need to select and **prioritize** your ideas to construct a piece of writing capable of influencing and convincing the reader.

Consider the following writing task:

> Your local newspaper is running a feature entitled 'Is it worth learning another language?' and has asked for readers to send in their views.
>
> You decide to contribute.
>
> **Write your contribution giving your views.** [20]

The opinions below represent possible arguments and viewpoints related to the topic of learning a foreign language. As you read them, decide which opinions you agree with and which ones, in your opinion, could form the basis of a convincing argument.

Key words

Prioritize – When it comes to transactional writing, 'prioritizing' means selecting the most important and the most relevant information and focusing on this first and foremost. What is 'most important' depends on the purpose and audience as established by the task. Keep the task in mind throughout and avoid getting bogged down with unnecessary details.

"People in other countries learn to speak different languages, which makes many British people look stupid..."

"Employers look for other languages when looking for their best candidate and the best-paid jobs are sometimes abroad..."

"Languages are fun to learn and can also improve your English writing and reading skills, which is a bonus..."

"Many people in Britain and America believe that everyone speaks English, but this isn't true, as not even a third of the world's population speaks English..."

"When you know another language, it makes it easier to travel the world and interact with other people, instead of shouting at them, hoping they will understand simple things..."

→ **CHALLENGE**

Choose one of the opinions and use it as the topic for a paragraph of four or five sentences. Then choose a second, related argument and do the same, making sure that this feels like a new point but follows the same line of argument.

Writing with maturity and control

High-level writing is characterized by maturity and control, so avoid gimmicks and overcomplicated vocabulary. Do not write for show. Sound control of words, sentences and paragraphs is what matters most.

Paragraphs should be varied in terms of length and structure in order to control progression. Vocabulary should be appropriate and should be chosen to convey precise meaning. **Stylistic devices** should relate specifically to the purpose and audience of the piece of writing.

> ### → CHALLENGE
>
> Read the opening to the welcoming 'speech' below. Choose a visitor to your school or college and write an opening to a speech to welcome him/her. The speech is going to be given during assembly to your year group, introducing the visitor.
>
> In your speech, explain why the visitor is regarded as a good role-model and the purpose for the visit. Write two well-developed paragraphs as an extended opening.

Year 11,

Today I am so pleased and proud to welcome Tom Daley to our school. He is here to talk to us and help us understand what it takes to be a champion.

Welcome to our school. We hope that you had a pleasant journey and we hope that during your stay you will enjoy what our school has to offer.

You have excelled in life and achieved many of the goals you set for yourself. You have inspired young people to concentrate on their education and to follow in your footsteps...

Writing with maturity is not only a question of style but also relates to the quality and substance of your argument, or the points you make in your writing. Read the opening to a phone-in contribution, below, on the topic of soldiers becoming teachers.

Today's phone-in: Should ex-soldiers be encouraged to teach in schools?
I say categorically 'no way!' School is already stressful as it is, but it is fun at times and it is about learning and being educated. It is no place for an ex-military officer. You can imagine the officer talking about life in the army and being determined to change the way students think with strict discipline. Every subject that a student takes will end up being related to the army. I don't want a school dominated by the military...

Key words

Stylistic devices – This really covers everything you do with language, from using metaphors and similies to wider persuasive techniques. The crucial point is that you use stylistic devices to achieve a specific purpose. Don't add them for the sake of it.

Avoid

Avoid slang as the norm. You should always aim to write in Standard English.

→ CHALLENGE

1. Write a contribution arguing the opposing viewpoint, in favour of ex-soldiers becoming teachers. Write two well-developed paragraphs.

2. Swap your work with a partner and use the **Upgrade** panel, below, to give your partner feedback on what works well and what could be improved in order to achieve a higher grade.

Upgrade

A* ↑	Paragraphs are effectively varied in length and structure to control progression. The writer has made confident and sophisticated stylistic choices, based on the purpose and audience. The writer has used a wide range of appropriate, ambitious vocabulary to create effects or convey precise meaning.
A ↑	Paragraphs have been used effectively to organize the content. The writer has used appropriate stylistic devices, which are closely linked to the purpose and audience. The writer has used a wide range of appropriate vocabulary that is ambitious but also accurate.
B	Paragraphs have been used to organize content and the writer has used fitting stylistic devices that relate to the purpose and audience of the text. The writer has used a range of appropriate and accurate vocabulary to convey meaning clearly.

Avoid ⚠

Avoid silly technical errors. Checking your work is a very good idea – try to make time at the end. Every error that you find and correct helps your cause.

As well as being marked in terms of how effectively you have responded to the task, you will also be marked on your technical accuracy. Technical accuracy covers everything from spelling, to grammar, to sentencing and paragraphing. It is vital that you are confident in these areas, if you are aiming for the top marks in this exam.

Building sentences and punctuating wisely

Sentence-building and punctuation are inseparable in many ways. Sentences should be controlled, but should be variable in length. Crisp punctuation is needed for sentences to work effectively, short and long.

At the top level, students will not only use punctuation with accuracy, but will also use it to create effects and avoid **ambiguity**. Read the start of the 'GCSE Survival Guide', below. This has been taken from an A-grade response.

> ### Key words
>
> **Ambiguity** – Something that could be understood in two or more ways – meaning that it is not clear to the reader. Punctuate your writing effectively to avoid confusion.

GCSE Survival Guide: How to survive your GCSEs this year

Hello everyone.
This article is for all you nail-biters out there who might be feeling a little overwhelmed by the prospect of starting Year Eleven in September. So don't panic! Here are some top tips for survival...

Be prepared

It is essential to start preparing for your exams in plenty of time so that you feel more relaxed and confident when the pressure starts to rise. After all, you don't want to be up till silly o'clock in the morning the night before your exam cramming in revision, do you?

Give yourself a break

There is no doubt that your GCSE year is going to be a very stressful and intense time of your life. (I know I wouldn't want to re-live it.) However, everyone needs a little break sometimes, so don't be afraid to just 'chill out' if you feel like your brain is frazzled.

Take it in your stride

I cannot stress how important it is to stay confident and not to go into meltdown when things go wrong. Believe me, it's not worth it! Try your best to make the most out of every situation, and if things don't go to plan, it will only make you a stronger person.

→ CHALLENGE

Add two more sections to the above (on topics such as food, sleep, study etc.). Use the same style of writing and make sure that your punctuation is part of that style, as it is in the response above.

Now read the opening to a letter on the next page. Complete one of the tasks that follow. Focus hard on punctuation control and selecting appropriate vocabulary. Ensure your spelling is accurate.

Dear Editor,
It has recently come to my attention that many people think that we should take holidays in Britain rather than travel abroad. I am writing to give you my views on this interesting topic.

Firstly, I would like to point out that I disagree entirely with the assumption that these people have made. For one thing, going abroad on holiday may well be considered 'expensive' during these economically challenging times, but going on holiday is Britain is hardly any cheaper. I went on holiday recently to the Lake District and it cost me a total of £400 to rent out a room for just three nights. How ridiculous! I would rather have spent that money on an exotic villa in lovely sunny Greece, wouldn't you?

→ CHALLENGE

1. Write two paragraphs that continue the pro-foreign holiday argument.
2. Begin a letter with at least two paragraphs that make the counter-argument for favouring British holidays.

Using correct spelling and grammar

Finally, do not be complacent about spelling and grammar. Proper proofreading is a good skill to have and a good habit to adopt. Avoid straightforward errors such as misused homophones or lack of subject–verb agreement. Be aware of word choice. Make sure you get the basics right but take responsibility for improving your ability to spell difficult words.

→ CHALLENGE

Read through all of the examples of student writing in this chapter.

1. List examples of word choices that reflect well on the writer's range of vocabulary and competence in complex spelling.
2. List examples of grammar (represented by phrases, clauses and sentences) that reflect well on the writer's mature use of style.

Demonstrating high-level skills

The following student response is based on a task that asks students to write the words of a speech. The task points out that the target audience is 'older people' and that the purpose is to 'persuade' them to put aside their concerns and start using computers and the Internet.

Read the response and the examiner comments that explain why this piece of writing is worthy of the highest marks.

Many older people don't use computers or the internet, either because they don't see any value in them or because they are afraid of modern technology. You have been asked to give a talk to a group of older people to persuade them to use computers and the Internet.

Write what you would say [20]

The quality of your writing is more important than its length. You should write about one to two pages in your answer book.

Quite a formal opening. It is very proper and not overly persuasive, but there is strong sentence control and a good, precise selection of vocabulary, which sets this piece of writing off to a good start.

The writing is rich in vocabulary and phrasing throughout; words are selected with maturity and precision.

Good morning, my name is Molly. Today I am here to talk to you about the joys of using the Internet. It isn't as daunting as you might think. The world of computers can open up new doors for you. Computers open the doors to new methods of communication, information and new friends.

I was very lucky; I was born in 1996 – around the time that the Internet was first being used. I grew up in a society where these modern technologies were the norm, and between my school education and my computer programmer father, I quickly learnt the basics of the Internet. Now, not everyone had that kind of upbringing and for people past a certain age, the idea of introducing this strange concept was, understandably, not going to happen.

Computers are pretty much essential in today's world, whether keeping in touch with friends, researching things for school or contacting people for work – it is all done on the computer. Although some choose not to, there is a reason that millions of people globally have chosen to give in to the power of modern technology: convenience!

You no longer need to wait days, or even weeks, for your friend to receive her letter in the post, you can just email her the very same message and it will arrive at her computer pretty much instantly.

This background makes the writing personal, which is not absolutely necessary, but does help to establish a rapport with the audience. It is engaging without losing the professional tone fitting to this subject matter.

This paragraph is a little more formal but just as controlled.

Engages the audience directly with a range of persuasive points. There are lots of arguments here that fit together cohesively, helping to build a strong case.

This paragraph deals with the question of expense and other practicalities, showing a level of maturity that adds credibility to the writing.

Have you ever not been able to remember the name of that one actor? Or forgotten the words to your once favourite song? I know I have! Websites like Wikipedia and Ask Jeeves are wonderful for speedily saving you from hours of frustration. Also, computer technology has advanced so much since the early nineties, that they are always getting faster and faster – no need to go and make a brew while you wait for the page to load. Brilliant!

You are never too old to start enjoying the world of the Internet! Can't see the point of computers? Neither did my grandmother. However, one day I took my computer along to her to show her how easy computing really is. She was soon starting research for a family tree, researching new recipes and playing bingo online while chatting to her brother in Australia over Skype. She now regrets not learning earlier, but stands testimony to how computing can change your life for the better.

You may think that owning a computer is expensive but according to Which? The consumer magazine, 'Computers are at the lowest cost they have ever been, thanks to competitive market rates' the magazine spokesman assured me. Computers can be used for free at most public libraries and a trained professional will be on site to help get you online. The government is even running a scheme to get older people online with special discounts on computing equipment and free training courses.

If you can take away anything from today's talk I would like it to be that you are never too old to get online! Within a few lessons you'll be surfing the Internet with ease! Who knows, maybe I'll meet you in cyberspace?

The tone is encouraging here and the example of the grandmother works very well to support this. The points made are all appropriately focused on the target audience.

There is no doubt that this is an excellent piece of writing that would achieve high marks, well into the A* band. As the comments around the response show, there are lots of things that this student does well. Crucially, however, the piece of writing is successful in that it remains committed to both the purpose and the audience throughout.

This piece of writing also demonstrates the need to provide substance in what is written. This student has definitely achieved that. There is an impressive level of information here and information and knowledge are vitally important when it comes to transactional writing. You need to be prepared to use your experience and your imagination to create content that is both appropriate and helpful to your cause.

The type and nature of information you choose to include will be directly connected to your **audience**. You need to think clearly about what your audience will already know about the topic and what they need to know.

Key words

Audience – The person or people you are writing to. Work out who your audience is before you write your response.

→ **CHALLENGE**

1. Look back at the speech on pages 66–7. Give some examples of information that the student has included to specifically appeal to her target audience.
2. Imagine you have to write an article about the 'Advantages of the Internet' for a teenage audience. How would this affect the information you would be likely to include?
3. What would your assumptions be in terms of their existing knowledge on the topic? What new knowledge/insight could you offer a teenage readership in your article?
4. Would this change of audience require you to change the angle of your writing and, if so, how?

The following activities give you a chance to practise your own transactional writing, taking into account the examiner feedback on the previous pages.

The government believes that we, as a country, need to be much better than we currently are at learning and speaking foreign languages. Many people believe, however, that 'everyone' speaks English as it is an international language.

A national newspaper is looking for young people to enter this debate. It heads this feature with the question: Is it worth learning another language? The newspaper is asking for articles that are both lively and serious about the value of trying to improve our awareness and grasp of other languages.

Write an article for the newspaper, as a young person looking to the future, giving your views on learning foreign languages.   [20]

You have a friend or relative who has asked you if you would like to go on a trip to London to witness the occasion of a royal wedding.

Write a letter to the friend or relative discussing the idea.   [20]

A leisure and travel magazine has asked for articles about places that offer a good holiday in Britain.

Write an article for the magazine that discusses the attractions of a place of your choice for a holiday.

You could choose one of the following:
- a town or city
- the countryside
- the coast.   [20]

→ **CHALLENGE**

Swap your work with a partner and annotate each response, adding comments highlighting strengths and weaknesses in the writing. Discuss your thoughts and comments with your partner.

Final word
What makes good transactional and discursive writing?

Good writing overrides labels. In fact, the official heading 'Writing about Information and Ideas' makes the challenge seem easier than it actually is. Writing factual information requires high-level skills of selecting, highlighting and prioritizing; personal ideas need to be well-judged, properly explained and sensibly sequenced.

In the exam you will be asked to produce two pieces of writing. You may be asked to write different types of texts such as a letter, an article, a speech and/or a leaflet. Matching your style to the format is key, but it is the <u>purpose</u> (what are you writing for?) and the <u>audience</u> (who are you writing to?) that are vital to the success of your writing. Consider the level of formality. Write brightly, but be sensible and serious where necessary.

Top students in the transactional writing exam need to have the poise to think and plan quickly. They need to grasp what the task requires and position themselves to make a case and to win the argument. Top-grade students write with impact, underpinned with a precise control of expression. They have a fluid understanding of formality and informality. They often display a variety of persuasive techniques, applying them with subtlety and authority and avoiding overbearing rhetorical skills.

Further task

You will have **one hour** in your exam to write a response to **two tasks**. The tasks will specify what form of writing is required and will also provide information about the purpose and audience of the writing.

Complete the following tasks as if you were attempting them in the real exam. You should aim to spread your time evenly between tasks.

---

*Answer Question 1 **and** Question 2.*

In this section you will be assessed for your writing skills, including the presentation of your work. Take special care with handwriting, spelling and punctuation.

Think about the purpose, audience and, where appropriate, the format for your writing.

A guide to the amount you should write is given at the end of each question.

1. A local adventure centre is seeking to recruit a part-time instructor to assist and supervise visitors. The centre offers activities such as rock climbing, caving and kayaking.

You decide to apply.

Write your letter of application.   [20]

The quality of your writing is more important than its length. You should write about one to two pages in your answer book.

2. Your school is considering whether to ban detentions on the grounds that they are not popular with students or parents. They have asked students to submit their views by email.

Write a response expressing your views.   [20]

The quality of your writing is more important than its length. You should write about one to two pages in your answer book.

Use the Upgrade assessment criteria, below, to rate your response to the practice tasks on page 70. Use the criteria to determine what you need to do to improve and write down three changes that could help you to boost your answer into the next grade band, or allow you to secure a stronger A*.

A*

1. Content is pertinent and well-judged, focused on the audience and purpose throughout.
2. The writing is cohesive and structured skilfully in order to influence the reader.
3. Arguments and ideas are convincingly developed.
4. The written style and choice of vocabulary are mature but fitting, and capable of managing irony.
5. Sentence structure and punctuation are expertly controlled to enhance the clarity and meaning of the writing.

A

1. The writing is clearly focused on audience and purpose throughout.
2. The writing is cohesive.
3. Arguments are pursued logically and fluently.
4. The written style is appropriate and there is a good range of vocabulary.
5. Punctuation is accurate and the writing shows skilful control of sentence structure and sentence variation.

B

1. The writing shows a clear sense of purpose and audience.
2. The writing is organized methodically.
3. Ideas and opinions are quite well developed.
4. Details are well judged and well selected.
5. The writing is competent technically.

Chapter 3.1

Speaking and Listening

Aim for A

- you are able to give a talk that is both lively and enterprising and you are able to engage your audience throughout
- you are able to make sustained and insightful contributions to class and group discussions
- in role-plays, you are able to create and sustain a convincing character in varied and challenging situations
- you are confident and accurate in your use of Standard English, your choice of vocabulary and your use of grammar.

Aim for A*

- you are able to give a talk that effectively persuades your audience as well as engaging them and holding their interest
- when giving your talk, you are able to handle a challenging topic, conveying your viewpoint confidently with expert knowledge
- you are able to lead a complex discussion effectively, directing it towards a positive outcome
- you are able to create and successfully sustain a demanding role, exploring complex issues both formally and informally from your character's perspective
- you are able to use appropriately skilful expression to convey and develop points in all situations.

Mastering Speaking and Listening

Speaking and Listening is more than just listening and speaking! If you are ambitious in your studies, both in English and in other subjects, you need to have a strong set of verbal skills. You need to be able to communicate effectively as an individual, work constructively with others, and deal promisingly with new situations. The real benefit of a good regard for Speaking and Listening is that it will reward you as a means of learning in other areas of the subject, and in other parts of the curriculum.

Can your spoken expression help you to write better? Can a dialogue with someone improve your understanding? Can you gain experience and learning about the world from a creative role-play? The answer to all of these questions is definitely yes.

Key words

Standard English – When it comes to speaking and listening, using 'Standard English' means avoiding slang and making a conscious effort to speak clearly, using the right words to suit the situation and your audience. It does not mean speaking laboriously in full sentences or eliminating all trace of any regional accent, but it does require precision and control.

THE ASSESSMENT

GCSE English Language Unit 4 Section A

Your Speaking and Listening skills will be assessed in three areas: communicating and adapting language (as an individual contributor); interacting and responding (in a pair or group) and creating and sustaining a role (in an unscripted situation). These tasks will be set up and marked by your teacher according to normal classroom practice. Your teacher may well have a role within the activity, perhaps as an interviewer or as a prompt for discussion.

None of the tasks should be scripted. However, preparation (including notes) for some Speaking and Listening tasks is a sound idea.

→ CHALLENGE

Discuss: Is speaking and listening just a one-sided competition between those who are confident and those who are not?

What you should and should not do

Do

- use **Standard English** in most situations.
- see beyond the obvious.
- try to win an argument by logical reason as well as forceful persuasion.
- enjoy what you are doing.

Don't

- try too hard to impress.
- rubbish other people's ideas.
- exclude anyone.
- underestimate the task.

Communicating and adapting language

Individual contributions, including talks, are better when they have a strong sense of purpose and audience. You do not need to use the traditional rhetoric of speech-making, but you do need to have eye-contact and a reasonably confident way of speaking.

> → **CHALLENGE**
>
> **Discuss:** What makes an interesting talk? Make a list of key ingredients.

Prioritizing information

Planning is essential. To achieve the highest grades you need to show that you can prioritize what you say; selecting the information that your listeners need in order to understand and appreciate your subject matter. Some speakers cram too much detail into thier presentations and risk confusing their listeners.

Your aim is to make a purposeful presentation while adhering to a strict time-limit.

> → **CHALLENGE**
>
> **ORGANIZE AND DELIVER A PRESENTATION TO BEST EFFECT**
> You will have **three minutes** to present a case for supporting your favourite charity.
> 1. Take no more than ten minutes to prepare your argument.
> 2. You will deliver your presentation to a panel of three other students who will <u>not</u> ask you questions, but who will decide how successful your talk is and will report back to you. The **Upgrade** panel, below, can be used for guidance.

Upgrade

A*↑	the speaker really persuaded me and I found the points made very convincing. The speaker seemed knowledgeable about the topic, the content of the talk was interesting and I felt engaged throughout.
A↑	the speaker made some strong points and the argument was very convincing. I also found the content of the talk interesting.
B	the speaker put forward a clear case, which was about the right length and was mostly interesting.

Thinking on your feet

You can't plan ahead for everything. Speaking and Listening is, after all, based on collaboration with others. You cannot always be sure how other people will react to you or what questions they might ask. However, top-grade candidates can really shine by showing that they can think on their feet.

Avoid ⚠
Do not try to memorize speeches for Speaking and Listening assessments.

→ CHALLENGE

LEAD A GROUP EFFECTIVELY TO AN END RESULT

Lead a small team in the production of a leaflet or brochure entitled 'A Guide to…' or 'A Beginner's Guide to…' or 'A Local Guide to…'. You will meet three or four times over a number of lessons. On the last occasion you will present your work to the class.

For this task you will be judged on the following:
- the way you organize your team
- the quality of the document the team produces
- the end presentation.

Using good English

Your choice of vocabulary and your use of grammar will be assessed as part of your performance in Speaking and Listening. To move up into the top grades you need to show flexibility and pertinence in your choice of words to best suit your topic and audience. Above all, you need to remain coherent and controlled when under pressure.

→ CHALLENGE

PARTICIPATE ACTIVELY AND COMPETENTLY IN A CHALLENGING INTERVIEW

You will be interviewed for a post that requires some management and leadership of people, including possibly people older than you.

You will be asked about:
- your personal qualities
- your skills and qualifications
- how you get on with people
- your ability to take responsibility and show initiative.

You might also be asked: how you would handle a professional disagreement; what kind of code of conduct you believe in and what kind of a role-model you would be for other people.

Interacting and responding

This part of your Speaking and Listening assessment will be based on pair or group work. It requires mature collaboration: working closely and supportively with a range of people.

Listening effectively

Most high-reaching students both enjoy group work and are good at it, but you do need to rein in your own views sometimes in the interests of others and you do need to listen well.

What makes a good listener? Here is what some other students had to say:

> *Somebody who doesn't interrupt.*

> *It annoys me when people look bored or when they just look blank, it really puts you off. It makes me forget what I'm saying.*

> *It's quite difficult to know how to balance encouragement and criticism. It's easy to upset someone and upset their confidence, but on the other hand they've got to listen to what I say too.*

> *Good listeners are people that ask questions that show they are interested in what you've said.*

→ CHALLENGE

Discuss the opinions above with a partner.
1. Which opinions do you agree with and why/why not?
2. What can speakers do to help their listeners be good listeners?

Key words

Active listening – Active listening is more than well-timed nods and sitting without slouching. At this level it means thinking while listening. You need to show that you are able to grasp complex ideas, pick out important points and build your understanding through asking insightful questions.

The highest marks for listening are awarded for being an **active listener**. This means that you are able to pay close attention to what is said and back up your listening with dialogue and questions that reflect your learning.

➡ **CHALLENGE**

LEARN QUICKLY BY LISTENING AND ENGAGING IN CRITICAL DIALOGUE

In a pair or a small group, study and discuss two unseen media texts in order to practise approaching and writing about similar texts in an exam.

You will need access to at least two pairs of texts to appreciate the range of text types and variation in subject matter that you might encounter in the real exam.

Resolving differences

Encouraging participation and resolving differences are vital to the success of any form of group work and this is true of the world beyond your Speaking and Listening assessment. These skills are important leadership skills and are used, for example, in teaching and when managing people in challenging situations.

Think ahead and develop your own strategies for dealing with situations such as:

- discussions where participants will not contribute
- discussions where it is not possible to reach an agreement
- discussions where other participants are preventing others from speaking.

➡ **CHALLENGE**

GUIDE AND TEACH A GROUP PROFESSIONALLY AND WITH ENTHUSIASM

Choose a small area of the curriculum that you excel in. Plan and deliver a teaching or coaching session for either your peers or younger pupils in which they actively participate and learn.

Make sure that you have an outline plan, with a beginning, middle and an end, and that you are aware of the time available and the time required for your lesson.

Shaping the direction of a talk

When working with others, students aiming for grade A* will show that they can influence how a discussion progresses by shaping the direction of the talk. To do this, you need to be flexible in order to develop ideas and challenge assumptions. You also need to be sensitive to the needs of the group as a whole. Your contributions need to be well-judged to support the aims and intended outcomes of the discussion.

> → **CHALLENGE**
>
> ### SUPPORT A CLASSMATE BY BEING HIS/HER 'COACH' AND CRITICAL FRIEND
>
> For this task you need to support your partner in the process of preparing and delivering a presentation.
>
> As a supporting 'partner', you need to contribute to the content and the style of his/her presentation. Set a high standard for your partner and be prepared to give constructive criticism.

Creating and sustaining roles

Role-play in Speaking and Listening does not require you to show acting talent in a play on stage. You do, however, need to consider different situations that you may encounter in real life in the future. It is about creating a convincing character that responds realistically to a given situation.

Creating a complex character

To achieve the highest grades you need to create a complex character and respond realistically to what other characters say and do within the role-play. Remember that your role-play will be **unscripted**, which means you cannot read from a script or learn 'lines'. You can plan the general content of the role-play in advance and it would be a good idea to do this, if you can, as a group. You can also research your character and spend time making yourself clear on your character's likely views and perspectives on issues that might come up in the role-play.

> **Key words**
>
> **Unscripted** – There are no scripts allowed, which means you need to think on your feet in terms of what to say during the role-play.

> → **CHALLENGE**
>
> ### ILLUSTRATE, THROUGH CHARACTER DEVELOPMENT WITHIN A GROUP PROJECT, ISSUES OF MANAGEMENT AND WORKING RELATIONSHIPS
>
> In a group of three or four, role-play a situation that illustrates constructively the difficulties connected with managing people sensitively in the workplace.
>
> You could use the role-play scenario given on the next page or create your own. You will then need to plan several stages of development for the role-play. You should allow parts for up to four characters (maximum) and there should be scope for complex interaction between them.
>
> Characters will need to be given a 'personality' and a 'brief', in advance, which clearly define the circumstances surrounding the events in the role-play. The role-play must not be scripted or over-rehearsed.

Role-play scenario:
Conflict in the workplace

Dilemma

Work situation. One member of a small office team is constantly late, takes personal calls and often leaves early. It is putting pressure on the other two members of the team and they are getting increasingly unhappy about it. They decide to complain to their manager, who then has to decide how to resolve the problem.

Characters/personality

- Boss Mrs Sutherland – very busy and overstretched; just wants to get things done as quickly as possible.
- Office worker 1 Olivia – 19-year old, first job, very able and friendly, caring personality.
- Office worker 2 Leo – 22-year old, just wants to get paid so he can party at weekends.
- Office person 3 Jane – 32-year old mum, very private person; her husband has just left the family home.

Brief

Mrs Sutherland – needs to sort out the situation and find out what the problem is in the office. Olivia and Leo raise the complaint. Mrs Sutherland has lots of other pressing matters to deal with but she is sensitive enough to know that the behaviour is out of character for Jane.

Olivia – wants to get on in her job but doesn't like the atmosphere in the office. She feels it is unfair but likes Jane.

Leo – big complainer and confrontational. He has made a complaint and wants to see something done to about it to reduce the burden on him.

Jane – has to explain her situation and is uncomfortable with both her situation and how it is affecting the job she loves. She is hoping for some help and support.

→ CHALLENGE

How does a good listener become effective at drama role-play? Discuss this question with a partner and create a list of tips and advice. Think about the need for listeners to remain in character as well as speakers.

Sustaining a complex character in varied scenarios

Sustaining a character means remaining in character throughout the task. This means you need to be flexible enough to respond to whatever happens in the role play as if you really are the character you are representing. To do this you will need to think on your feet, as well as keep track of everything that your character has said and done so far during the discussion. Your character needs to have a 'memory' so that what they say and do is consistent with what has already taken place.

The next task follows on from the task on pages 78–9 and asks you to adopt the same character in order to reflect on your behaviour and actions during the previous task.

> ### → CHALLENGE
>
> **REFLECT IN ROLE THE CONTRIBUTION MADE BY YOU AND OTHERS IN A PROJECT**
> Hot-seat one of the four characters created in the world of work role-play that you set up on pages 78–9. Reflect on your actions and behaviour and that of the other characters involved.
>
> Your character should show some self-awareness and show credible understanding of the other characters.

Responding to a literary text

Can good speaking and listening benefit your understanding of literature? Here is what some other students had to say:

❝Yes, having a dialogue about the texts we are studying lets you say the things you want to say, rather than spotting things you think you're supposed to notice. It sort of gives you confidence for when you have to do it alone in the exam.❞

❝I don't think so, speaking and listening is all about opinions and to really understand literature you have to stick to the facts.❞

❝Yes – asking questions helps you to check your understanding and to test out ideas.❞

❝Yes – hearing what other people think about literature helps me to focus on what I really think.❞

> ### → CHALLENGE
>
> Look at the opinions, above, from students. Do you agree with all of these comments? In a group of three or four, discuss each opinion critically and decide what you would add or what you disagree with completely.

At least one of the Speaking and Listening tasks that you will be assessed on will be based on a literary text that you have studied. This is an excellent opportunity to make sure you know your stuff for your literature exams. You don't have to know exact answers – you just have to be able to think on your feet and be able to discuss sensible possibilities. Attempt the task below with a partner, based on one of the writers you are currently studying. Once you have carried out one interview, swap roles, so that both of you have an opportunity to role-play the writer and the interviewer.

→ CHALLENGE

ROLE-PLAY AN INTERVIEW WITH A WRITER OF ONE OF YOUR LITERATURE SET TEXTS

Hot seat William Shakespeare or another writer that you are studying on your English Literature course.

Be prepared to develop answers to challenging questions about the play or novel, the motivation of the characters, and the intended meanings and outcomes of the story.

Final word

What makes 'top' students in Speaking and Listening?

Perhaps the key quality they need is 'quick thinking' because nothing should be scripted. You need to be able to lead on occasions, but also be a good team member, who listens to others. Whether you are working on your own, in a team or as a team-leader, you need to complete the task set, in a way that resolves a situation. Speaking and Listening should be more than hot air!

Good speaking and listening comes with some hard work. You should make the most of all opportunities you get to practise and improve your skills. Be active in reviewing your strengths and weaknesses. What verbal skills inside and outside the English classroom have you been able to develop in the last year or so? Consider the opportunities that you have had in other parts of the curriculum and in the world of work and the community.

Good speaking and listening skills are important for life; for further education, university and beyond. Think ahead. What verbal skills are you going to need in the kind of job you would like to have?

A further set of tasks

All of your Speaking and Listening work will be assessed by your teacher. You may participate in many Speaking and Listening activities throughout the course and your teacher will select which ones will count towards your final GCSE.

The tasks that follow provide three opportunities for you to practise your speaking and listening skills, while being reviewed by one or more of your peers. You will have an opportunity to listen to their feedback before carrying out your own review of the work presented by other students. Use the **Upgrade** assessment criteria on page 83 to help you assess the work of your peers and to put together constructive feedback that will help them achieve their full potential.

INDIVIDUAL TALK: DELIVER A PRESENTATION TO WIN A VOTE

Your school is hosting a party for school leavers and the head teacher would like to put together a committee of four students to help plan the event. All students who would like to be involved are required to give a five-minute presentation. You need to explain what you could bring to the committee and what, in your opinion, is vital for a successful party. Once all the candidates have presented, students will then vote for the representatives they would like to see on the committee.

GROUP/PAIR WORK: DEBATE ABOUT THE MORALITY OF A CHARACTER IN A LITERARY TEXT

Select a character from a text you are studying, who could be perceived as good or evil, based on his or her actions in the text. Get into groups of eight, with four students representing one perspective and the other four representing the alternative perspective. Spend some time selecting evidence from the text that might be useful to support your case. Carry out the debate as a group, aiming to hear everybody's point of view and to consider the key arguments in some detail.

ROLE-PLAY: A RADIO PHONE-IN ABOUT A LOCAL ISSUE

A local radio station is hosting a phone-in for residents, entitled "Is it time to give in?", about the intended sale of a section of forest by the government to a manufacturing company that is planning to open a large production plant there. There have already been a series of disorderly protests around the site, with people chaining themselves to trees and chanting slogans. Two weeks ago a passer-by had to go to hospital after a placard was apparently thrown at her by one of the protestors.

Two people will be needed to play the parts of the radio show presenters. Other students should take the roles of different callers. Each caller should state who he or she is when the call is answered and may make up to two calls each.

Use the marking criteria below to assess your partner's performance in each of the practice tasks on the previous page. Work out what your partner could do to improve in order to move up into the next grade band.

A*

Individual talk

1. Does the talk suggest that the speaker can deal with complex and demanding topics successfully?
2. Does he/she speak with assurance by manipulating language confidently?
3. Does he/she keep the audience genuinely interested throughout and possibly persuade them?

Group/pair work

1. In collaborative (pair/group) work, does the speaker contribute fully, with skill and authority?
2. Does he/she listen perceptively and with concentration, even in challenging situations?
3. Is he/she able to show skills of leadership, resolve differences and achieve a positive outcome?

Role-play

1. Does the speaker create a complex role convincingly?
2. Is he/she able to adapt speech subtly to suit the formality/informality of the role?

A

Individual talk

1. Can the speaker cope with complex topics and deliver a talk confidently?
2. Can he/she organize and sustain a response fluently and coherently under some pressure?
3. Can he/she adapt comfortably to a range of situations when called upon to talk?

Group/pair work

1. Does the speaker contribute consistently and positively to the group task?
2. Does the speaker show that he/she is a patient and supportive listener?
3. Is he/she able to take the lead in a group situation, if required?

Role-play

1. Does the speaker create and sustain a role convincingly?
2. Is he/she able to respond effectively to changing situations while remaining in role?

B

Individual talk

1. Does your partner speak purposefully and confidently to the audience?
2. Is he/she able to organize the talk and cope with challenging questions?
3. Is he/she consistently effective with the use of Standard English?

Group/pair work

1. Is your partner able to make reasonably significant contributions to the discussion?
2. Does he/she listen with a good level of concentration?
3. Does he/she reflect, clarify and question constructively within the group?

Role-play

1. Is your partner able to tackle a fairly challenging role with some confidence and success?
2. Can he/she deliver a role informally but effectively?

Aim for A

- the spoken language study will be detailed, with thorough coverage of the transcript and a sensible selection of examples and comments
- the study will show a good grip on the context of the transcript
- the essay will be fluent, coherent, sustained and organized.

Aim for A*

- the spoken language study will present a consistently persuasive answer to the question
- the essay will give the reader a very clear sense of the context of the transcript
- the writing will give the impression of maturity and authority, from start to finish.

Studying spoken language

Spoken language is a part of day-to-day life and to study spoken language you need to make the most of all of your experience of using it yourself, reacting to how others use it and viewing it via the media. There is no difficult expert language to learn. We are all capable of being experts on spoken English.

Spoken language, not surprisingly, is closely linked to Speaking and Listening and your Speaking and Listening work may help to inform your studies in this part of the course. Equally, the study of spoken language should contribute to the improvement of your verbal skills.

In your final written study, you will be expected to **analyse** spoken language – this means nothing more than 'to examine in close detail'. You are expected also to **evaluate** spoken language – this means making judgements on the quality and success of people's use of spoken language.

You 'analyse' and 'evaluate' in other areas of English, notably when writing about literature. What is the main difference here? The main difference is that spoken language is like a moving target. A transcript helps you pin it down a little, but good analysis and evaluation of spoken language also considers how speakers move, how they sound and how they behave.

Key words

Analyse – To examine in close detail. When writing a study of a text or a piece of spoken language, this means looking at what is said and also <u>how</u> it is said.

Key words

Evaluate – To make a judgement on the quality and success of a person's use of language. For example, if the speaker is aiming to persuade listeners, does the speaker succeed in convincing them?

THE ASSESSMENT

GCSE English Language Unit 4 Section B

This unit will be assessed by Controlled Assessment. You will be required to study an aspect of spoken language. The assignment will be a written response to your own or others' uses of spoken language.

Your study may be based on a recording, a transcript or your recollections. You will write your essay under controlled conditions and you will have **two hours** to complete it. Your teacher may decide to split your writing time into shorter sessions. If this is the case, you must hand in your work at the end of each session.

In preparation for the Controlled Assessment, you will work on the task in lessons, probably annotating a transcript and gathering notes. As with other Controlled Assessments, you will know the question before the final writing sessions begin. The study is worth 10% of your overall GCSE English Language qualification.

Unscripted speech

You should aim to base your study on unscripted, spontaneous speech. Spontaneous spoken language is spoken language that isn't learned in advance or read out. Admittedly, some performers are very good at disguising their careful preparation and planning, but they get the benefit of the doubt if they appear to be speaking naturally!

Scripted speeches and dialogues can be used in your spoken language study – but <u>only</u> if they are being compared with extracts and examples of spontaneous spoken language.

Using transcripts of spoken language

It is a good idea to use a transcript (or transcripts) as the basis for your study.

A transcript is a written representation of spoken language. The study of spontaneous spoken language includes such features as pauses, interruptions and other items that tend to occur in speech, but not in writing. However, the transcript is not expected to be technical; it is enough for the words and features to be accurately transcribed with appropriate punctuation.

Below is an extract from a transcript of the television programme *The Apprentice*.

The Apprentice

Interviewer: So how have you got on with the other contestants?

Contestant: I have found it very, very hard.

Interviewer: There have been some comments that they find you rather cold, detached, stand-offish.

Using a transcript will benefit you because you will have something to refer to in detail when writing your study. If you also have a recording or video of the speech to refer to, remember that the speaker's **body language** and how the speaker sounds, are also valid things to comment on and should not be ignored!

Key words

Body language – This might include any aspect of the speaker's behaviour that relates to what is said or how it might be interpreted. It includes movement, eye contact and facial expressions.

How long should a transcript be?

A one-page transcript might be long enough, but will require some very detailed study to produce an essay of the required length. Some students have successfully used transcripts as long as four or five sides of A4 paper. A longer transcript such as this would allow you more scope to select and highlight the key points that you would like to focus on in your essay. A short transcript of one side would be of most use as part of a comparison task.

Who 'writes' the transcript?

There are no marks for actually writing a transcript at GCSE. Furthermore, if you as a candidate make a poor choice of topic and text, it will cost you marks! In practice, your teacher will most likely determine the task for your whole class and may also supply you with one or more transcripts. It is not a bad idea, however, to gain some experience of making a transcript as part of your learning and preparation.

Spoken language case study: *Dragons' Den*

Dragons' Den is a BBC TV series in which business hopefuls try to promote their ideas to a panel of five wealthy investors. Contestants make a pitch for financial investment, offering a stake of the company in return. The rules say that, if they do not raise the full amount they need from one or more Dragons, they must leave with nothing.

The TV programme *Dragons' Den* offers various topics that could be studied in relation to Spoken Language, such as the world of work or the world of the media, and also how speakers react to the demands of tough questioning and the need to think quickly.

Clarity and persuasion are the key linguistic skills required on the show, but if the product or the business skills are poor, the contestant has little chance of success.

Read the sample assessment task below and work through the activities that follow. The task and activities require you to watch a full episode of *Dragons' Den*.

> Watch a one-hour episode of *Dragons' Den* and track what you can learn about business, language and how the speakers react to one another.
>
> What do you learn from watching the episode about the way people speak and behave?

Comparing speakers

In a one-hour programme, there are usually four contestants who are featured in detail. Other, normally unsuccessful contestants, are shown briefly in between the main features. There may be just one or two entrepreneurs who are successful in any programme.

→ CHALLENGE

As you watch the episode, collect a list of reasons why various contestants failed to persuade the dragons to invest.

A contestant speaks for one or two minutes to the five judges or 'Dragons' about his or her ideas. Most of them have a product on display, and some try gimmicks to attract attention. Some make a heavily prepared pitch and are too nervous to remember what to say; others have a much more natural style of delivery.

→ CHALLENGE

Write two paragraphs comparing a good presentation with a not-so-good presentation.

Techniques of questioning

When the presentation is over, the Dragons take over as an interviewing panel, asking some searching questions, which are intended to test out the quality of the contestant and the product.

→ CHALLENGE

Over the hour-long programme, make a note of tactics and attitudes adopted by the different Dragons.

Negotiation and agreement

When individual Dragons decide they are not interested in the business proposition they say "I'm out!" Often, all the Dragons are like-minded, and quickly withdraw, sometimes gently, sometimes with quite strong criticism.

In cases where Dragons are interested in the product, negotiations take place, in order to try to reach an agreement. There is often haggling between the contestant and the Dragons, and sometimes amongst the Dragons.

→ CHALLENGE

Note any points of interest in the way negotiations take place.

In the response below, a student has chosen to focus her study on one contestant from *Dragons' Den*. This is a borderline A/A* grade answer.

→ CHALLENGE

Read the response and the questions given in the margins. Work through the annotations, answering the questions as you go.

Is this a useful introduction for the reader? What could make this introduction more helpful to readers unfamiliar with Dragons' Den?

Does this paragraph tell us enough about Shannon's presentation?

Does the writer's use of 'paralinguistically' impress or not? What does it mean?

How does Shannon Richards make a winning pitch in Dragons' Den?

Shannon Richards is a 24-year-old woman who is trying to secure some money for her company 'Sweetsons' on Dragons' Den. Dragons' Den is a popular TV show, where five multimillionaire businesspeople invest their money in members of the public that need money in their businesses. Shannon is trying to get one or more of the 'Dragons' to invest in her dairy-free dessert for children.

When the show starts, Shannon's demeanour is naturally modest and polite. She has a reassuring voice, looks cheerful and is smiling, possibly because she is nervous. The viewer's first impression is that Shannon is working class, with a northern accent, and is not very business-like and she is not going to win. During her fluent, well planned opening, she becomes more confident and shows the viewer that she knows what she is talking about, with expert knowledge about things such as "Manuka honey" and "Echinacea". Her modesty and politeness are shown in phrases such as "thank you" and "sorry", which she uses frequently.

The Dragons respond to Shannon's pitch paralinguistically. To start off with, they are sat back in their chairs and one of them is laughing. They then try her product and sit there tasting it. It is obvious that they have accepted her product taste-wise because they continue eating it until they have finished. Later, as they warm to Shannon, they smile at her and ask her questions. Then, when she says that she has been talking to Tesco about this, they all sit up amazed.

Shannon shows a good knowledge of her product and shows that she has researched it well. When she is asked questions about it, she comes straight back with detailed, extended answers. For example, when she is asked, "what are the ingredients in this?" she comes straight back with "it's made with brown rice milk… apple, carrot and grape". This highlights the fact that she is sure of herself and she is explaining the reasons further. She is quietly confident about this and handles the questions smoothly, replying back almost immediately. She is a good speaker, and has eye contact with the person she is talking to. This can be hard for her, especially when the interrogation is from everyone, not just the one person at a time.

The writer is now in her stride and writing well. Discuss the merits of this paragraph.

Shannon's responses to the questions are straight to the point. When asked "how much has it cost you to set this up?" she replies "about twenty thousand". She could have replied back with a woolly answer, such as "well, it cost me ten thousand the first month, seven thousand the second month…" but she chooses to be straight to the point, which probably increases her chances of getting the investment. Shannon's product is already a winner before she opts into the 'Dragons' Den', as she demonstrates there is already a market for this product. She says "I'm starting to get into bigger places with it" and this is confirmed when she says later that the supermarket Tesco want to put this product into a "minimum four hundred stores from September, when they do the refresh". This had an effect on the Dragons and probably made them think that Shannon's product was worth investing in.

This paragraph is a little less convincing, although the points are still relevant. What is it that makes it is less convincing?

Shannon has a tremendous amount of knowledge and has some past experience also. She knows what she is talking about and this helps the Dragons to make a decision whether to help her. She knows all about her product and the benefits it has on people, such as "it's ideal for coughs and colds" and "all our products are low in calories". Her personal experience shows when she says "organic virgin coconut oil that I personally test". She is also passionate about her product, as she says "I had to leave...really believed in it". This is made personal by the fact that she was inspired by her "four year old child who has dairy intolerance". This also shows her love and passion behind it.

This paragraph is quite relevant and moves the essay forward quickly. Comment on what makes it effective.

In this interrogation, there are many fillers such as "erm", "like" and "oh, basically". These show where the speaker is giving herself time to think and to process the information. There is also a bit of slang, such as "uni" and quite a lot of pauses, where again the speaker is thinking or digesting the information. The longest pause is when Shannon is talking about the "big supermarket". Those pauses are mainly to let the speaker and listener think about a fact, or from Theo to Shannon; and this was to let her get prepared for a question.

How useful is this paragraph on fillers?

Pick out some good-quality phrases from this paragraph.

The Dragons are curious as to Shannon's product. They ask her many questions, such as "how much has it cost you to set this up?" This shows their interest in the product and that they want to know more about it. The questions get fired at her after the first part and she answers smoothly and quickly, with little hesitation. The pressure intensifies against her here, as she is getting more questions fired at her all the time. The Dragons are trying to catch her out, as they ask difficult questions.

In what ways could this paragraph be improved?

Shannon's story unfolds as the Dragons ask more questions. The Dragons want to know whether Shannon is telling the truth, testing her the whole time and picking points she has mentioned. They ask her to expand on them, like "this big supermarket that you've talked about?" She proves to them that her story is true, as she says things that a person who didn't know about this wouldn't use or understand, such as "when they do the refresh". After Shannon has said what the supermarket is interested in, the tone of the conversation becomes more interested and the firing of questions slows down. This is where the Dragons are warming to her and she is no longer selling her product to some disinterested customers; they are now buying her product because they are interested in it. This shows that her pitch certainly is a winning one, although there is still a long way to go before they make their bids.

The essay on *Dragons' Den* is clearly a fluent, sustained effort, showing a comfortable understanding of the way the programme works and, on this particular occasion, why the contestant, Shannon Richards, is successful.

Is the answer confident and sustained?   **Yes**
Does it answer the question?   **Yes**

Does the answer show understanding of variations in Spoken Language?   **Perhaps**
Does it evaluate the impact of Spoken Language choices?   **Perhaps**

> **CHALLENGE**
What could this student do to improve the answer to secure a grade A*?
Use the **Upgrade** panels, on the next page, to help you.

Upgrade

UNDERSTANDING VARIATIONS IN SPOKEN LANGUAGE	B	→ A	→ A*
How does the essay deal with the content and development of Shannon's talk and the purpose of it?	clearly and accurately	with detail and understanding	fluidly, with insight and understanding
Does the essay focus on the specific situations that Shannon faces, such as the questions and negotiations?	yes – mentions situations	yes – focuses on the range of situations	yes – understands impact of the range of situations
Does the essay consider the identity of the speaker?	yes – on a basic level	yes – refers to speaker's situation and aims	yes – refers to personality, mood and knowledge of topic

Upgrade

EVALUATING THE IMPACT OF SPOKEN LANGUAGE CHOICES	B	→ A	→ A*
Does the essay judge Shannon's use of persuasive language and its effects?	yes – identifies persuasive techniques	yes – identifies techniques and judges effects	yes – critically evaluates Shannon's performance
Does the essay identify the different stages of Shannon's pitch to the Dragons?	yes – identifies some progression	yes – identifies how pitch changes as it goes on	yes - understands how Shannon's pitch changes as it goes on
Does the essay draw out the attitudes of the interviewers?	yes – considers interviewers' reactions	yes – identifies reasons for interviewers' reactions	yes – effectively differentiates between interviewers

The conclusion that you should have reached through this step-by-step assessment is that the essay is indeed a good one, but that the answer to some of the questions listed above is not conclusively 'Yes'.

The strength of the essay seems to be how well this student has engaged with the contestant and her situation and how well she has understood the task and the event. The relative limitation of the essay appears to lie in the lack of explicit analysis and evaluation of Shannon's language. In a way, this contestant is quite difficult to analyse because she is successful in her pitch; perhaps, after all, an unsuccessful pitch to the Dragons might produce more critical analysis.

Nevertheless, this level of response deserves great credit and reaches towards the top bands of the mark scheme – therefore not full marks, but still arguably in the top band of marks.

Writing about variations in spoken language

Writing about variations in spoken language means showing an awareness of how spoken language is used, selected and adapted. Within any five-minute extract of unscripted speech, you are likely to find evidence of speakers adapting their speech to meet the shifting demands of the dialogue.

For example, if a speaker is asked a question, the expectation is that the speaker will provide information. If a speaker is interrupted, the speaker will need to re-assert themselves in order to get their point across.

→ CHALLENGE

Consider each of the situations below. Drawing on your experience of spoken language as both a speaker and listener, in what ways might these situations affect the way people use spoken language?

> The speakers do not know each other very well, having only met once before.

> One speaker seems visibly upset by something another speaker has said and begins to cry.

> There is one member of the team who is much more senior than the other team members, with the final say in terms of decision-making.

> A speaker is giving instructions to a group of five other people, who seem to be getting confused and are having trouble keeping up.

Variations can occur very quickly within a free-flowing discussion, affecting the structure of the dialogue and also the language used. Be attentive to the details: specific word choices can reveal a lot about a speaker's intentions, priorities and his or her relationship with the other speakers.

→ CHALLENGE

Read the comments below from other students about spoken language choices. Which points do you agree with and why? Be prepared to discuss your answers with the class.

66 People think less about their choice of words when they are speaking in comparison to when they are writing. 99

66 Choosing the right word is less important when speaking because you can correct yourself or check if people don't understand. 99

66 The words people use in unscripted speech can give away secrets about them that they might not want people to know. 99

66 It's possible to tell if one person likes another person just by the words they use. 99

Final word

What makes a good spoken language study?

A top-grade spoken language study will offer confident analysis in this new subject area. It will be free from technical clutter, but will demonstrate control of a ready vocabulary to handle concepts and situations in the working language of the world of work and the media.

A student aiming for the top grades needs to show that he or she can sustain a written response impressively without losing sight of the question. He or she will be able to detect tone, mood and atmosphere with confidence and will be able to recognize how these change as speech progresses.

Above all, he or she will have grasped the idea that spoken language is a 'moving target'. In the case of a transcript, students aiming for the top grades need to understand that the written words on the page are only part of the spoken language that they are studying. Spoken language is made up of words, volume, movement, silence and visual elements. All of these factors are important in terms of the way human beings interpret spoken language.

Further task

The practice assessment task below provides a good opportunity to write an essay on spoken language study and then self-assess it, in order to identify where you have scope to improve. This activity is based on *Dragons' Den*, but a similar format could be applied to many other television programmes, where unscripted spoken language is a focus and a big part of the entertainment value.

Analyse and evaluate **two** bids for the Dragons' business support. Compare and contrast the effectiveness of the two bids.

You should consider:
- the way the bids are presented initially
- the response to the Dragons' questions
- the attitude of the individual Dragons
- any other areas of interest, such as negotiations and disagreements.

Remember to look closely at the way language is used.

Remember also to draw upon your wider understanding and experience of the programme, and the world of work and the media.

Upgrade

Use the marking criteria below to assess your response to the practice task on page 94. What grade do you think you are likely to achieve with your response? What could you add to or remove from your essay in order to improve it and boost it into the next grade band?

A*

1. Does the response successfully re-create the drama and occasion of the original spoken language text to a great extent?
2. Does the answer select, highlight and prioritize the important details confidently?
3. Has the answer been written with authority in a way that analyses and evaluates spoken language as a 'moving target'?
4. Have you sustained a clear and coherent argument throughout?

A

1. Have you written a thorough response to your chosen spoken language text?
2. Does your response contextualize the focus of your study?
3. Does the response demonstrate a regular balance of detail and overview?
4. Have you been able to transfer key reading and writing skills from the study of literature to create a strong, convincing essay?

B

1. Is your response sustained and organized?
2. Does your essay include plenty of relevant detail?
3. Does it give a sense of the context of the focus of your study?
4. Is your answer clear and credible throughout?

Acknowledgements

The publisher and author would like to thank the following for their permission to reproduce photographs and other copyright material:

p6: richardarno/iStock; **p8:** David Davis/Shutterstock; **p9:** Celso Diniz/Shutterstock; **p10:** Graeme Robertson/The Guardian; **p13:** DNY59/iStockphoto; **p15:** Anton Gvozdikov/Shutterstock.com; **p16:** greenland/Shutterstock; **p19:** domhnall dods/Shutterstock; **p20:** domhnall dods/Shutterstock; **p22:** Morey Milbradt/Alamy; **p25:** The Moviestore Collection Ltd; **p29:** NBC Universal; **p31:** Nick Scott/Alamy; **p38:** Eric Broder Van Dyke/Shutterstock; **p40:** Lukasz Misiek/Shutterstock; **p41:** Rtimages/Shutterstock; **p42:** Stuart Crump HDR/Alamy; **p44:** David H.Seymour/Shutterstock; **p45:** Old Visuals/Alamy; **p47:** Rex Features; **p49:** eyed/Shutterstock; **p50:** Viktor Gladkov/Shutterstock; **p52:** Dan Briški/Shutterstock; **p53:** A ROOM WITH VIEWS/Alamy; **p56:** ThomasSaupe/iStock; **p58l:** Yuri Arcurs/Shutterstock; **p58r:** Tracy Whiteside/Shutterstock; **p60:** Getty Images; **p61:** Franziska Lang/Shutterstock; **p65t:** Kevin Eaves/Shutterstock; **p65b:** Maugli/Shuttertsock; **p68:** Monkey Business Images/Shutterstock; **p72:** Paul Frederiksen/Shutterstock; **p75:** Kzenon/Shutterstock; **p77:** lightpoet/Shutterstock; **p79:** iofoto/Shutterstock; **p84:** moodboard/Alamy; **p86:** Christopher Halloran/Shutterstock.com; **p87:** Rolf Marriott/BBC Photo Library; **p88:** Yuri Arcurs/Shutterstock.com; **p94:** 1000 Words/Shutterstock.com.

Illustrations by Rory Walker.

The author and publisher are grateful for permission to reprint the following copyright material:

Bill Bryson: extracts from *The Life and Times of the Thunderbolt Kid* (Black Swan, 2007), reprinted by permission of The Random House Group Ltd. **Laura Clark:** 'Class atten-shun! How ex-soldiers could be deployed as teachers', *Daily Mail*, 15.2.2008, reprinted by permission of Solo Syndication/Daily Mail. **Bruce Chatwin:** extract from *On the Black Hill* (Vintage, 2008), reprinted by permission of The Random House Group Ltd. **Francis Gilbert and Adnan Sarwar:** 'Should more ex-solders become teachers?', *The Guardian*, 24.11.2010, copyright © Guardian News & Media Ltd 2010, reprinted by permission of GNM Ltd. **Bel Grant:** 'Have a Grumpy New Year Everyone', *The Weekly Gripe* 6.1.2011, reprinted by permission of the author. **Stuart Maconie:** extract from *Adventure on the High Teas* (Ebury Press, 2010), reprinted by permission of The Random House Group Ltd. **Meera Syall:** *Anita and Me* (Flamingo, 2001), copyright © Meera Syall 1996, reprinted by permission of HarperCollins Publishers Ltd. **Alexandra Topping:** 'Action for Happiness movement launches with free hugs and love' *The Guardian*, 13.4.2011, copyright © Guardian News & Media Ltd 2011, reprinted by permission of GNM Ltd. **Wikitravel:** extracts from article on São Paulo released under the Creative Commons Attribution 3.0 Licence, http://creativecomons.org/licenses/by/3.0.

Although we have made every effort to trace and contact all copyright holders before publication this has not been possible in all cases. If notified, the publisher will rectify any errors or omissions at the earliest opportunity.